W9-CSJ-842

Nov 2, 1998

Dear Francis,

It was a pleasure to have you visit Gracie. Thank you for the wine. A toast to your next NY film!

Warm regards,

Donna

Mary Black

New York City's Gracie Mansion:
A History of the Mayor's House

an account of the years 1646 to 1942 based on *Gracie Mansion:*
An Historic Structures Report by Joan R. Olshansky, Former Field Director
for Brooklyn, Queens, and Staten Island of the New York City
Landmarks Preservation Commission, and on the unpublished
manuscript by Susan E. Lyman, "Archibald Gracie and his Mansion"

Published for The Gracie Mansion Conservancy
by The J. M. Kaplan Fund, New York, 1984

Library of Congress card catalog number: 84-15445
ISBN 0-9613729-0-7 cloth edition
ISBN 0-9613729-1-5 paper edition

Foreword

Not only is New York City my home: my home is New York City's. I have lived in Gracie Mansion since 1978. When I first moved in, I thought, "What a wonderful house – and it's all mine!" However, it didn't take me long to learn that it would also be my pleasure to share this remarkable residence with tens of thousands of official guests and visitors every year. On many occasions, I have personally conducted tours of the house and grounds and have given impromptu lectures on the mansion's long and interesting history.

Now Mary Black has made it possible for everyone to enjoy an expertly guided tour of Gracie Mansion. This book will allow the reader to learn more about the origins and many lives of this extraordinary part of New York and American history. I greatly appreciate the excellent work of the Gracie Mansion Conservancy, under the direction of Joan K. Davidson, in this endeavor.

The Conservancy, with advice and assistance from design and preservation experts, is helping to provide the necessary repairs and improvements which will preserve the house as a building of prime civic importance and pride.

To know the history of Gracie Mansion is to know the history of New York, the most exciting city in the world. As you begin this book, therefore, the world is – in a very real sense – at your fingertips. Welcome to Gracie Mansion!

The Honorable Edward I. Koch, Mayor, New York City

Introduction

First of all, Gracie Mansion is home for New York mayors and their families.

But it is more than that.

Gracie Mansion is also an historic place and a symbol central to the lives of New Yorkers. The mayor's house serves as an extension of City Hall where much city business goes on: a lively, varied procession of official events and the comings and goings of community leaders, members of civic and trade associations, state legislators, foreign dignitaries, New York City officeholders—about 22,000 guests each year. In the mansion public policy often takes shape and the spirit and verve of the city are always manifest.

New York is the only American city that keeps an official residence for its mayor. But Gracie Mansion, built almost two centuries ago, was for most of its years in private hands; of New York's 105 mayors, only the last seven—from Fiorello H. LaGuardia, beginning in 1942, to Edward I. Koch—have lived there.

Like the city it represents, the mansion has been transformed over the years. Archibald Gracie, the first owner, was a leading citizen of early New York and an active player on the stage of the young republic. In 1799 he built a modest house on the ruins of an earlier one and during the next eight years added a parlor and upstairs bedrooms.

In the house he entertained illustrious Americans, from Alexander Hamilton to President John Quincy Adams, and foreign notables including the Marquis de Lafayette. Later owners added porches to the house and moved doors, fireplaces and staircases about, altering and realtering the interior design. The city claimed Gracie Mansion in 1896 and alternately used and neglected the house until, in the days of the New Deal, Robert Moses remodeled it and the mayors took occupancy. Mayor Robert F. Wagner changed it once more, adding a wing in 1966.

So the original house survives. Having comfortably accepted the rearrangements and accretions, it has held on through the generations to remind us of New York's phenomenal growth since the 1700s. In a sense, the history of the house is the history of our city and of the nation as well.

And the process of change goes on. Modifications needed in our own time to assure the continuing vitality of the house, in both its working and its ceremonial aspects, are being guided by the newly formed Gracie Mansion Conservancy.

Established by Mayor Koch in 1981, the Conservancy is a not-for-profit corporation, a public/private partnership that will stay in business through succeeding mayoral administrations. Its mission is to repair the structure where needed, to enhance Gracie Mansion's position as New York's first house and to provide for the long-term preservation and well-being of the entire property, the better to serve the people of the City of New York.

Leaders of New York's museums, libraries and historical societies, and the New York Landmarks Preservation Commission and the Department of Parks and Recreation are among the Conservancy's trustees and advisors. A team of talented professional architects and designers has been engaged to renovate the exterior, interior and landscape. Following the Mayor's example, the Conservancy is expanding public access to the house through a series of tours, cultural events and educational programs, of which this publication is an early product.

Many hands have contributed to this book by Mary Black. Professional staff members of The New-York Historical Society helped her create an important show there in the winter of 1981–82: *The Mayor's House—Gracie Mansion and Other Dwellings*. This exhibition turned up a surprising store of information about the old house—portraits of those who lived there, objects they owned and paintings, photographs, maps and prints recording the appearance of the site throughout its history. Mrs. Black's book incorporates this material, along with much of two unpublished biographies of Archibald Gracie by Susan E. Lyman and information from an Historic Structures Report on the mansion and its site by Joan Olshansky, published by the New York Landmarks Preservation Commission.

Two grants have made this publication possible: one from Joseph B. Martinson Memorial Fund (through the interest of Paul and Frances Martinson and Howard Graff); the other from Foundation Krikor (through the interest of Ralph Esmerian).

James J. Heslin, former Director of The New-York Historical Society, supported initial plans for the book. Larry Sullivan, the Society's former Librarian, provided a permanent home there for Susan E. Lyman's manuscripts. Thomas J. Dunnings, Jr., Curator of Manuscripts, suggested manuscript sources concerning Archibald Gracie and others, and journals and papers dealing with the construction of City Hall, which was completed in the same period as early additions to the mansion. Mary Alice Kennedy, Registrar of the Society's Museum, prepared most of the captions for the book's illustrations and in other ways provided invaluable support for Mrs. Black's efforts. M. J. Gladstone read the text and gave critical comments that have been valuable in establishing its content and form. Vignelli Associates, and in particular Peter Laundy of that distinguished firm, created the book's design. The Publishing Center for Cultural Resources is responsible for its production.

The Conservancy believes that if this book can encourage New Yorkers to care about the vivid history of Gracie Mansion, it may do even more—deepen their pride in the great city itself. To this end Mary Black's erudite and charming account of the early Gracie Mansion story makes an important contribution, and I join the Mayor in saluting her for it.

Joan K. Davidson, Chairman, Gracie Mansion Conservancy
February 1984

Contents

Illustrations

3

This book is dedicated to Susan E. Lyman

Susan Lyman, one of the best informed of New York's modern historians, wrote and lectured frequently about the city's culture and many charms; she wrote pamphlets on the city's manners and on one of its early historians, Martha J. Lamb. Two books demonstrate this dedication: The Face of New York: The City As It Was and As It Is, *with photographs by Andreas Feininger, published by Crown in 1954. Ten years later, also published by Crown, was her last book* The Story of New York, an Informal History of the City. *Miss Lyman spent years in tracing and writing the history of Mr. Gracie and his country seat; her two manuscripts on these latter subjects, labeled "dead hopes," were among the papers left for disposition by her literary executor, Mrs. David S. Wells, and were made available to Mrs. Olshansky and to the author by Mrs. Wells.*

New York City's Gracie Mansion:
A History of the Mayor's House

Prologue: Horn's Hook, 1646–1798

Before the City of New York secured possession of Gracie Mansion in 1896, ownership of that point of land on the East River had been, since Colonial times, in the hands of only six men and their relations by blood and marriage. For more than three centuries, only two dwellings of any significance have stood on the site. The second, rising on the foundations of the first, has stood for more than half that time.

In the spring of 1646, shortly before the arrival of Peter Stuyvesant as the Dutch West India Company's Director-General in New Amsterdam, his predecessor, Governor Willem Kieft, granted 15 morgens of land at Hell Gate to Sybout Claessen. On that same day Claessen was allowed two lots within the village of New Amsterdam at the southern tip of Manhattan: one of them, with a house and garden, on the east side of Broadway near Wall Street, the other at the southwest corner of Stone and Whitehall Streets. Claessen, a carpenter, lived in the village. Using his upriver land as a farm, he named it Horn's Hook after his native town of Hoorn on the Zuyder Zee in the Netherlands.

Thirty years later, as New Netherlands passed for the second time from Dutch to English hands, ownership of the farm went from Claessen to one of the founders and a large landowner in the township of Harlem, Barent Resolved Waldron. Waldron's daughter Cornelia, and her husband, Pieter Van Obliensis, lived in a farmhouse at Horn's Hook for a brief period. Shortly before the 1689 ascension of William of Orange and Queen Mary to England's throne, the first of five exchanges of the farm within the Waldron family took place.

In September 1770, in the year in which New Yorkers and British soldiers had already come to blows in the Battle of Golden Hill, William Waldron's widow and her son sold a little less than seven acres of the land at Horn's Hook to Jacob Walton for just under £440. For five shillings more, Walton purchased the right of way for a road 20 feet wide west of the hook. Less than a month later, Walton added approximately four acres to his Hell Gate property, completing assembly of the plot of 11 acres that was to become Archibald Gracie's country seat and that is today (excluding the early right of way) the official residence of New York's mayors and the northern portion of Carl Schurz park.

Jacob Walton's purchase was only a small part of the Waldrons' extensive holdings in New Harlem. But then, as now, it was the choicest: a high promontory of land looking out to the turbulent waters of Hell Gate where a rocky cliff makes a steep drop down to the river. The river inlet at the north, the original boundary of Horn's

Hook, had a gentler slope, and it was here, in waters calm after Hell Gate's churning, that fish and oysters abounded. Walton's purchase was from the present 86th Street to just above 89th Street east of East End Avenue. The right of way was on a line with 86th Street and extended from the river plot to midblock between present-day York and First Avenues, where it joined the meandering road to Hell Gate Ferry.

Ten years before this purchase, Jacob Walton, a successful young member of a New York merchant family, married Polly Cruger, joining fortunes with another great merchant family. Years later, this Hell Gate landowner was identified as "a magnate of the days when merchants were Princes in New York." The year preceding his acquisition of Horn's Hook land, Walton had been elected to the General Assembly along with John Cruger, his wife's uncle. (England had disenfranchised the previous New York Assembly in 1767. That step and heavy additional taxes levied by the mother country led to the dissolution of the earlier assembly.) On April 5, 1768 John Cruger, Jr., New York mayor from 1757 to 1766, led a group of friends, including Walton, in organizing the New York Chamber of Commerce. Cruger became president of this, the first mercantile association in America. In the midst of the Revolution, with New York in English and Loyalist hands, Jacob Walton was twice elected vice-president of the Chamber—in 1781 and 1782. As a Loyalist, Walton joined his fellow merchant, James Delancey, in advancing money for shipping and in erecting the statues of King George at Bowling Green and William Pitt at the corner of Wall and William Streets. Both works, by British sculptor Joseph Wilton, were destroyed early in the Revolution—George III toppled from his perch on July 9, 1776, and Pitt losing his head in November 1777.*

Pieces of the George III statue are in the collections of both The New-York Historical Society and the Museum of the City of New York. Also in The Society's collection is the headless form of Pitt.

Shortly after his 1770 land purchase, Walton built a mansard-roofed, double-chimneyed house with one-story ells at each end, at the highest elevation on Horn's Hook, overlooking a lawn gently sloping to the rocky point overlooking Hell Gate. In anticipation of the coming struggle between Loyalist and Patriot that was to divide the city and its merchant families, he built an underground tunnel as a means of escape to the river. Before 1776, Walton also built the structure a little removed from the waters of the inlet; beside it was a separate but closely sited low structure with a shed roof. Access to the secret passage appears to have been from these buildings as well as from the house.

Much later, in 1913, the foreman of Carl Schurz Park found an underground passageway, its walls lined with brick, that led "north

Map of Harlem

Print drawn and published by James Riker in his *Harlem Its Origins and Early Annals*, 1879

This map of Harlem, by its early historian James Riker, shows the area's original lots and farms. "The 10 Lots" at Horn's Hook and the three adjoining lots south of them, lower left, encompass the entire extent, and more, of the 11 acres on the East River successively owned by Jacob Walton, Archibald Gracie and Joseph Foulke. The owners of a much larger farm at the period illustrated were all members of the family of Resolved Waldron and included, at various times, his sons, sons-in-law, a daughter-in-law and a grandson. The original grantee was the Manhattan carpenter Sybout Claessen, who used it as his farm, naming the point Hoorn's Hoeck after his native city on the Zuyder Zee.

"Waldron Farm at Horne's Hook."

From *Abstracts of Farm Titles In the City of New York* by Henry C. Tuttle (New York, 1878) opposite p. 97.

Overlaid on the early nineteenth-century Manhattan Street grid are the outlines of the 115-acre Waldron farm. The land, including the right of way to Hell Gate Ferry Road that was Archibald Gracie's, lies directly on the East River at Horn's Hook, center far right, north of the ferry house at 86th Street. Here it is marked as belonging to "William Waldron, afterwards Jacob Walton, afterwards Joseph Foulke," omitting Gracie's ownership from 1799 to 1823.

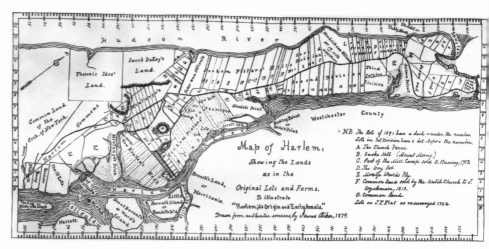

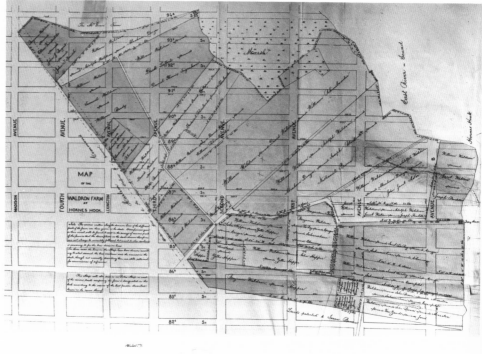

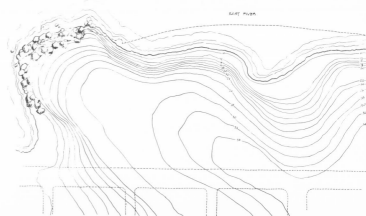

Gracie Mansion Restoration:
The Site—1676.
Pen-and-ink drawing by Philip N.
Winslow, Landscape Architect,
September 1981.
This is a conjectural contour drawing of the
site of Gracie Mansion as it is likely to have
appeared in the seventeenth century. The grid of
New York streets, from 86th to 89th Streets
(as they intersect at East End Avenue) and the
present shoreline are indicated by dotted lines.

*"Map of New York I. with the adjacent
Rocks and other remarkable Parts of
Hell-Gate."*
Pen, ink and watercolor by Thomas
Kitchin, Sr., ca. 1776.
*In this map by the "Hydrographer to his
Majesty," Thomas Kitchin, Sr., there are
several errors in both the land and water areas
surrounding Long Island Sound, Hell Gate,
and the entrance to Harlem Creek. Although
Horn's Hook and the battery opposite Hallett's
Point are correctly sited, Blackwell's and other
river islands are either diminished or
exaggerated. It is, nevertheless, useful in
showing principal land and water routes and
the small town of New York at the very tip of
the island. The map also settles the matter of
the tavern later mentioned as being on
Walton's land. Shown here as being
immediately north of Horn's Hook, it is
identified as "Walderon's Tavern."*

9

for some distance" and then turned east and continued to the water's edge. Parks Commissioner Charles B. Stover theorized that

the passageway was constructed for the purpose of effecting a secret escape from the house in the event of it being surrounded by enemies. Such necessity might have impended at the time of the Revolution, when the British held the city and their warships covered the East River and neighboring waters.

The New York Sun report continued:

By means of this tunnel it would have been easy for the endangered persons in the old mansion to go down to the river and take a boat over to Long Island, which is but a short distance away at this point. A man could row from the park over to Steinway now in half an hour.

A Gracie descendant, Miss Edith Gracie, strengthened the supposition, noting that

the existence of the underground passageway had been a tradition in the family in the later generations. It had been constructed at the time of the Revolution and was intended as a quick way to reach the boats at the river's edge in case of sudden danger to the inmates.

Before the Revolution broke out in New York, Walton's Loyalist sympathies led to action supporting the British point of view. He and John Cruger wrote in 1775 to General Gage in Boston, informing him of the state of affairs in New York and entreating him to withhold sending troops against New Yorkers loyal to the king.
Early in April 1776, Washington ordered General Charles Lee to New York to prepare the town's defense against the British. But even before fortification of Manhattan, American rebels had appropriated the Walton house. In the words of a contemporary:

you may recollect a sweet situation at Horne's Hook that Jacob Walton purchased, built an elegant house, and greatly and beautifully improved the place.
He was obliged to quit as troops took possession and fortified there. When Mrs. Walton received the order to go out of her house she burst into tears, for she was fixed to her heart's desire.

Part of the American defense was the construction of two opposing forts, at Hallett's Point in Queens and at Horn's Hook, to block the hazardous passage at Hell Gate. In late February 1776, batteries rose at both sites, as Samuel Drake's Westchester Minute Men began construction of the redoubt on the west shore. This was Thompson's

10

Battery, named after patriot General William Thompson, made to accommodate 300 men. There were four six-pound guns and four 12-pound guns in place "behind Mr. Walton's house at Horn's Hook facing the East River," an indication that the main entrance to the house faced the lane rather than the water.

As Washington arrived in New York to take command on April 13, 1776, Isaac Bangs, a second lieutenant in the Second Militia Regiment of Barnstable County, Massachusetts, commented on the vista on sailing down the East River:

. . . we set sail about 1 o'clock . . . about 2 o'clock we arrived at Turtle Bay, between Hell Gate and New York. Here we were obliged to tarry till the next day . . . for Orders. On both sides were many very elegant Country Seats, & at Hell Gate a handsome and well-constructed Fort lately built by our people. Near this place are several elegant and beautiful Country Seats, Several evacuated by the Tories. I visited the Garden of one Gentleman in which was a Summer House which the Gardener showed me . . . many curious Flowers, &c.; but the greatest Rarity was Orange, Lime, Pomgranet, & Citron Trees all Bearing Fruit.

On September 8, after several days preparation in placing mortars and heavy guns, Archibald Robertson, British "engineer extraordinary and Captain-Lieutenant," directed the bombardment of the rebel works at Horn's Hook from Hallett's Point. Ironically, it is Robertson's drawings of the site, immediately before and after the bombardment, that are the only records of the appearance and outline of Walton's house.

Excerpts from Robertson's diary for that month tell of the preparations and of the bombing:

. . . reconnoitred the shore opposite Hell gate where the Rebels have a Work round Walton's house, call'd Horn Hook, the water or East River about 500 Yards across here . . .
2nd sent early to General Clinton about placing mortars to drive the Rebels from their work at Walton's house. Nothing done . . .
4th Evening Captain Moncrief and I were ordered to raise two batterys at Hell gate against Walton's House . . .
A working party of 300 men. We began to work at 1/2 past nine and by 5 next morning they were completed within 2 hours work of 60 men. This Evening a Party was sent to raise a Breast Work on Blackwell's Island, to drive the Rebels from their work at Walton's house. Nothing done . . .
10th this morning the light Infantry took Possession of Bahanna's and Montresor's Islands with the loss of one man Killed and one Wounded.

11

(above)

"View of the Opening of Our Battery's at Hell Gate, upon the Rebel Works at Walton's House."
Watercolor by Archibald Robertson (ca. 1745–1813), September 8, 1776.
The view is northwest from Long Island. To the north (at right center ground) is Hallett's Point; across the East River is Walton's house and the American battery at Horn's Hook—the future site of Archibald Gracie's country seat.

12

(top right)

"View of Part of the Rebel Works Round Walton's House with the situation of our Batterys on Long Island ..."
Watercolor by Archibald Robertson (ca. 1745–1813).
This view is southeast from the vicinity of present-day 92nd Street. To the south, at center right, is the fort at Horn's Hook (located on Walton land); to the east is the British battery at Hallett's Point. The structure in front of Thompson's Battery is thought to be Walton's stable and small barn with a carriage shed behind it.

(center right)

"View of the Rebel Works Round Walton's House with Hell Gate and The Island."
Watercolor by Archibald Robertson (ca. 1745–1813), October 8, 1776.
The view is from the American battery at Horn's Hook, on Walton land looking east to Hell Gate and Long Island. Mill Rock is at middle ground, to the left of the flagpole. From the drawing close at hand of the ruins of Walton's house, the landscape and preservation architects of the Gracie Mansion Conservancy have been able to reconstruct the plan of the first house on the site.

(bottom right)
The Site—1776.
Pen-and-ink drawing by Philip N.
Winslow, Landscape Architect,
September 1981.
The conjectural drawing by Philip Winslow
for the Gracie Mansion Conservancy is based
on Archibald Robertson's long-distance and
close-range drawings of the Walton House and
the Revolutionary fortifications at Horn's
Hook.

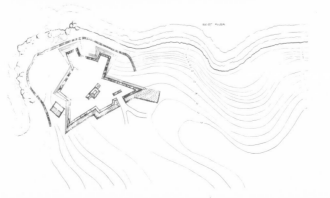

13

*The Rebels by our Preparations think a landing intended near Walton's
House. This Day they are Busy throwing up Breast works along the
shore . . .*
*{September} 16th in the morning visited the Rebel work at Waltons house. We
might have storm'd it in front, if it had been required, as it was greatly
Destroyed by our Batterys. The Parapet of 11 feet thick resisted our 24-
Pounders at 710 Yards Distance. We had 130 Wounded and 8 Killed.
The firing lasted for some hours . . .*

The Americans had evacuated Thompson's Battery as the British
advanced, and the abandoned fort was soon occupied by a British
party led by Lt. John Heinrichs. Just after Robertson's inspection,
Heinrichs wrote that he had established headquarters "100 yards from
Hornhogk on the East River." As he marched up the island to the
American battery, he kept close to the river and reported that the
shore was "lined with the finest houses. I had the pleasure of taking
all these houses together with [the] hostile battery where I found 5
Cannons."

As the British continued to break through Patriot defenses to occupy
New York early in October 1776, Walton joined other Loyalists in a
petition to Lord Howe, commander of British forces in the city. Years
later, when claims were presented to the British for retribution, John
Harris Cruger, Walton's brother-in-law, set the damage to the house
at a little over £1700, a figure that appears to indicate total
destruction of a sizable dwelling. While only the foundations of the
house remained, the British occupied the land at Horn's Hook until
Evacuation Day, November 25, 1783.

After being forced from their "heart's desire," Jacob and Polly Walton
joined other Loyalists in Queens. On August 1, 1782, Mrs. Walton
died there, within eight days joined in death by her husband. Their
estate was left in equal shares to one son and three daughters. Sixteen
years after their parents' death, the descendants still retained
possession, until December 29, 1798, when three-fourths of Jacob
Walton's land was sold to Archibald Gracie of New York, "merchant."
Two weeks later, in an arrangement with Gerald Walton, one of his
brother's executors, the remaining share of the Walton tract became
Gracie's. The 11 acres at Horn's Hook cost $5625.

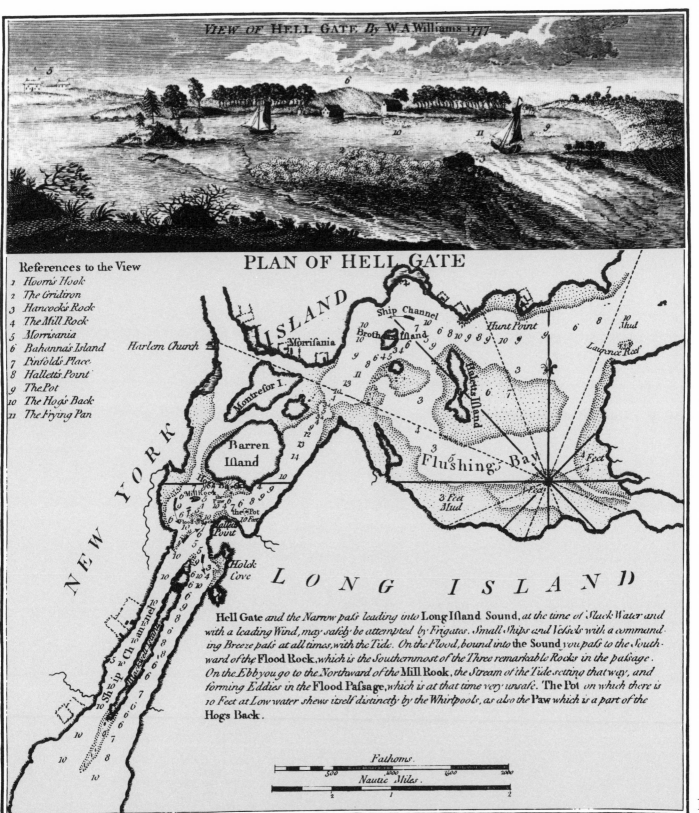

"East View of Hell Gate, in the Province of New York."

Print published in the *London Magazine*, April 1778, from a drawing by William A. Williams, 1775.

The original of this charming vista, past the churning waters of Hell Gate, was drawn at the rocky heights of Horn's Hook in 1775. Loyalist Jacob Walton still occupied his house there before being, "obliged to quit . . . the sweet situation at Horn's Hook" as it was fortified by American Minute Men.

East View of He...

1 *Hoorn's Hook*.   3 *Hancock's Rock*.   5 *Morr*
2 *The Gridiron*.   4 *The Mill Rock*.   6 *Baha*

lliams del. 1775

7 Pinfold's Place.   9 The Pot.   11 The Frying
land.   8 Hallet's Point.   10 The Hogs back.   Pan.

Archibald Gracie and His Country Seat at Hell Gate, 1798–1823

Archibald Gracie, son of a Scots weaver, was born in Dumfries, Scotland, on June 25, 1755. He turned 21 as the American Revolution was declared and as he joined the Liverpool office of the large West India shipping house of Reid, Irving & Co. of London. Within five years, Gracie was chief clerk; by 1784 he had outside accounts of his own and was part owner of the ship *Jeanie*.

Five months after British forces evacuated New York, Gracie arrived in the city on the *Jeanie*. Its entire cargo, consigned to Gracie, contained, among other goods: plain and figured kentings, durants and tammies; watches; tin and Japanned ware; china, earthenware, and pewter dishes; Cheshire and Gloucester cheese; and "fine London Porter and Liverpool Beer." On his arrival in this country he immediately formed a mercantile company, with Freeland and Muir of Liverpool and Andrew Muir of Norfolk, Virginia, as his partners. On May 15, in New York's *Independent Journal*, Gracie announced "excellent accommodations for passengers" on the *Jeanie* to Liverpool via Norfolk, Virginia. The goods he had on consignment were "to be sold from on board the same ship, laying at Commissaries wharf." By early June he was installed in a house and shop at the commercial center of the city at No. 224 Queen (now Pearl) Street. The conclusion of the same advertisement demonstrates fulfillment of his intention (stated in a letter to England of this period) to rent two of his rooms at Queen Street, "suitable for a single gentleman."

By summer's end, the difficulties of selling quantity lots on credit in New York, and the lure of enormous profits on importation of Virginia tobacco "sold at retail," without "the ruinous custom of giving credit," drew him to Petersburg, Virginia. There, with Andrew Muir and others, he established import businesses in tobacco and European goods; later he founded Gracie Anderson and Co., which eventually became one of the largest companies of its kind in the South.

Gracie's mercantile affairs brought him to New York frequently, and on one of these trips he met the three Rogers brothers—Moses, Nehemiah and Henry—city merchants and grandsons of Thomas Fitch, Connecticut Governor from 1754 to 1766. Their sister, Esther, or Hetitia, also lived in New York. Early in 1785 New York was named the first capital of the United States, and in September of that same year, Archibald Gracie married "the amiable Miss Hetitia Rogers on Queen Street." The couple had met at Moses Rogers' house at No. 272 Queen Street, between Fulton and Beekman (in a house that Susan Lyman, Gracie's biographer, characterized as "a commodious place of unusual charm with a hanging garden that extended out over the yard and stables and offered a good view of the East River"). The newlyweds traveled to Virginia to live; Gracie had earlier purchased land there and later bought an adjacent lot, presumably as the site for a house.

In Petersburg, Gracie at once became part of the busy port's civic and church life: in the eight years that it was his home he was successively alderman, vestryman of Bristol Parish Church and, in 1792, a member of the city's Common Council. Four of the couple's eight children were born there: Margaret (who died young) in 1786; William on November 28, 1787; Eliza on September 6, 1789; and Sarah Rogers on December 14, 1791.

Early in 1793, perhaps in acknowledgement of his wife's close family ties, Gracie returned to New York with his family. For the rest of his life the city was to be his home and business headquarters. The family rented a house at No. 110 Broadway, located, Lyman notes, "just a short block north of Wall Street and almost opposite Trinity churchyard, the mayor of the city, Richard Varick, becoming his landlord and neighbor."

In the years that Gracie had been in Petersburg establishing an international mercantile business, Lyman continues,

New York was on its way to becoming the business center and main port of the country. Pearl, Water and Front Streets, together with the wharves and slips along the East River, were the heart of this pulsing development. Here one saw the constant movement of merchandise as cargoes were transferred between ships, nearby warehouses, and stores.

The year before Gracie's return, a group of brokers met to form what was to become the New York Stock Exchange. The three Rogers brothers were in business in the city and although Gracie was to have continuing business and social ties with them and with their brother-in-law, David Lambert (the husband of Elizabeth Rogers), he went into business for himself as a commissary merchant, using his home as his office. The extent of his many interests is indicated by his fleet of ships. Between 1784 and 1808 he owned at least 21 cargo-carrying ships, brigs and schooners built in Massachusetts, Maine and New York. The goods of his highly successful Virginia enterprise were shipped to New York, reloaded there onto larger ocean-going vessels and sent on for sale to English and Dutch merchants. Gracie arrived at a fortunate time. In 1797, as John Adams became the nation's second president, New York achieved first place in American shipping; the value of the city's exports was $13.3 million, more than five times their value in 1792. Although he never held political office in New York, Gracie allied himself with the Federalists, the party of Richard Varick and his brothers-in-law. The "Famous Four" of the

20

Federalists—Alexander Hamilton, Rufus King, Gouverneur Morris and John Jay—were his friends and associates in a variety of business, social and civic enterprises.

Soon after his return, Gracie became a shareholder in the Tontine Association of New York merchants, in 1794 installed in its second building at the northwest corner of Wall and Water Streets. Within the confines of The Tontine Coffee House, the city's banking, insurance, civic and charitable enterprises were organized and conducted. Archibald Gracie became an active participant in many of these transactions.

In the spring of 1795, as he joined the Marine Society, Gracie was also elected to membership in the New York Chamber of Commerce, and from 1800 to 1825 was its vice-president. In the fall of 1796 he joined his fellow Scotsmen and became a member of St. Andrew's Society. At the turn of the century he was its second vice-president and its president from 1818 to 1823.

In the spring of 1797, Gracie joined the Sub-Rosa Club, a gentlemen's social group. Among the many guests that Gracie introduced to fellow members at their three o'clock turtle and oyster dinners was Alexander Hamilton, on August 25, 1798. In 1796, Gracie was made president of the New York Insurance Company. Two years later the company, with offices at No. 66 Wall Street, was incorporated with capital of $500,000 to handle maritime insurance and insurance for "houses, goods, and lives." First in 1797 and frequently thereafter, Hamilton represented Gracie and his company in a variety of court cases involving shipping. At the end of the eighteenth century, as Dr. David Hosack, a fellow Sub-Rosa Club member, organized the Lying-In Hospital, one of the first—and one of the largest—contributors to the hospital was Gracie, who served on its board of governors from its founding to 1824.

On the final day of 1799, a public ceremony was arranged honoring the memory of Washington, who had died on December 14. Gracie was one of three Chamber of Commerce members chosen to draw up a resolution for the ceremony. He marched in the procession that Lyman describes as

A seemingly endless line {that} wound its way through the city streets. Military units, artillery captured from the British during the Revolution, crepe-decked members of all the leading societies (Gracie could have marched with half a dozen of these). Behind them came national and state officials, then the musical groups with "twenty of our maidens" in white robes scattering laurel leaves in front of the elaborate funeral bier.

Almost a year to the day before this event, on December 29, 1798,

The Tontine Coffee House.
Oil on canvas, by Francis Guy, ca. 1798.
*Located on the northwest corner of Wall and
Water Streets, the Tontine Coffee House (at
left) was erected by the Tontine Association in
1792–93. Archibald Gracie, a backer of this
organization in 1793 and 1794, owned a
share in the association. As a businessman
with many concerns, Gracie was a frequent
visitor to the Tontine Coffee House. Of the
activity there John Drayton wrote in 1793,
"From eleven to two o'clock, the merchants,
brokers, etc. meet at the Tontine coffee-house,
. . . where, they transact all their concerns in
a large way, and where, the politics of the day
are considered. Here, the insurance offices are
kept: blank checks on the different banks are
ready for those who may want them, and
everything in the busy line transacted." Two
books were also kept here, "as at Lloyd's, of
every ship's arrival and clearing out."*

**Northeastern Corner of Wall and
William Streets, 1798.**
Watercolor by Archibald Robertson
(1765–1835), 1798.
*The three buildings illustrated in this turn-of-
the-century watercolor are, from left to right:
The Bank of New York, No. 32 Wall Street;
the New York Insurance Company, No. 34
Wall Street; and the Bank of the United
States, No. 38 Wall Street. In 1798
Archibald Gracie became a director of the
Bank of New York, joining Rufus King and
his two brothers-in-law, Moses and Nehemiah
Rogers. (King's sons, James Gore and Charles,
later married Gracie's daughters.) In 1798
Gracie became president of the New York
Insurance Company, and on May 14, 1805 he
was elected a director of the Bank of the
United States.*

Archibald Gracie had made his first purchase of land at Horn's Hook to become the fourth and, until mid-twentieth century, the most famous of the owners of this site; an additional purchase completed the East River plot for his mansion. Modern archeological tests show that Gracie's original house there was a two-storied, double-chimneyed structure. There were probably two rooms on each side of a central hall on the first floor, and three bedrooms, a storeroom, and a closet on the second. The main entrance faced east to a vista identical to that seen in the "View of Hellgate," an aquatint engraving published in London in 1807. The house rose over the foundations of the main part of the Walton house destroyed by the British shelling in September, 1776. A turn-around carriage drive led visitors to the front door. The leveled Revolutionary fort provided the flat base on which the new house was built.

It was probably under construction when, early in the month of Washington's death, a sensational murder was disclosed when the body of Gulielma Sands was found in the Manhattan Company's well near Spring Street. The suspect was Levi Weeks, who, with his brother Ezra, sons of the cabinetmaker Thomas Weeks of Greenwich, Massachusetts, designed and built a number of houses in New York (as well as the stout wood surround of the well where the body was found).

The case came to trial on March 31, 1800, the result of a murder indictment against the suspect brought by a grand jury of which Archibald Gracie was foreman. The trial itself produced a number of curious alignments: among those presiding at the Court of Oyer and Terminer was Mayor Richard Varick, Gracie's landlord. Cadwallader Colden, later to be mayor of the city, was assistant attorney general and served as prosecuting attorney. The three defense lawyers were Alexander Hamilton, Aaron Burr and Brockholst Livingston. The most complete account of the trial itself—but not of the grand jury's preceding indictment—is by William Coleman. The result of the murder trial, bolstered by Burr's careful defense and unassailable evidence of Weeks' innocence, led to the suspect's being declared "not guilty" by the jury after only five minutes deliberation. Both Ezra Weeks and John McComb, Jr. (the builder of City Hall and one of its architects) testified compellingly for the defense.

In building his country seat in 1802 and 1803, on the south side of present 143rd Street west of Convent Avenue (later moved to a new location on the east side of Convent Avenue between 141st and 142nd Streets), Alexander Hamilton used Ezra Weeks as chief builder. Rufus King, father-in-law of two Gracie daughters, also employed Weeks in adding to his country house in Jamaica, Queens. As early as 1799

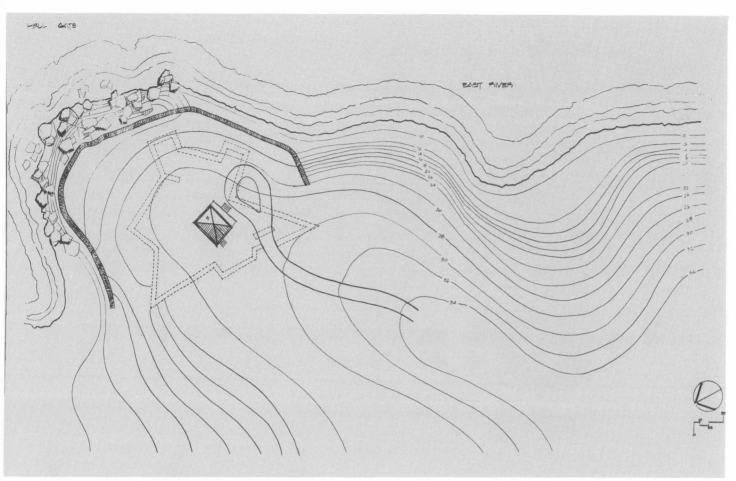

HELL GATE

EAST RIVER

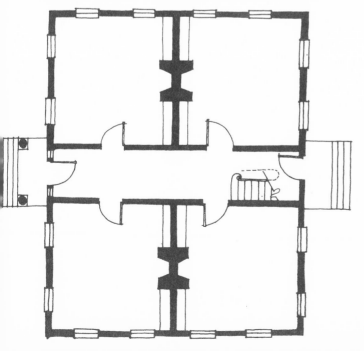

25

Weeks was in business for himself in New York, listed as a "builder" at a Greenwich Street address. Miss Lyman suggests that he was the craftsman most capable and most available as the builder of both the original house and the additions to Gracie Mansion in 1799 and early in the nineteenth century. The circumstantial evidence of this and of a later acquaintance with Gracie appears to strengthen this theory.

In 1800, as the population of New York went over the 60,000 mark, William Coleman, chief chronicler of the Sands trial, became editor of a Federalist paper founded by Gracie and friends; the *New York Evening Post* made its first appearance on November 16, 1801, emanating from a Pine Street office provided by Gracie. In 1801, the year of Jefferson's inauguration as third President, Esther, the last of the Gracies' children, was born in New York (Mary, born in 1793, died young; Alexander, Jr., was born in 1795; and Robert in 1799). The following year Gracie's house at Horn's Hook was finished, identified as "land and house" on that year's tax list.

As construction of the country seat went forward uptown, Gracie moved his downtown office. For the three months between November 1800 and January 1801 he advertised his office location at No. 156 Pearl Street above Hone's Auction House; but in mid-November 1801, in announcing a new office location, he mentioned that his business address was being changed from his "dwelling house" to No. 52 Pine Street.

At the suggestion of Alexander Hamilton, his successor as Secretary of the Treasury, Oliver Wolcott was put forward for a partnership with Gracie and three of his brothers-in-law. Like Wolcott, the latter were part of the exodus of men from Connecticut to New York. All the partners in the new enterprise, except Gracie, were from Connecticut: the three Rogers brothers, Moses Rogers' brother-in-law, William W. Woolsey, and his next-door neighbor, James Watson. Wolcott was the salaried head of the firm and the other partners each put $15,000 into the business. All shared in the profits. Among the company's clients were three other New Englanders: George Cabot of Boston, John Brown of Providence and painter John Trumbull, then in London. Eventually, these commission merchants established accounts with Baring Brothers of London, Hope & Co. in Amsterdam and Preble & Co. in Le Havre. (The first two had enjoyed business dealings with Gracie since 1785.) Gracie and his partners were soon seeking contacts in Spain, Portugal and Italy, as Wolcott wrote to the former U.S. minister to Spain late in 1805, proposing "promising speculations" to the Mediterranean in West Indian produce and in Haitian coffee. In

City Hall, New York, Front Elevation and Cross Section of Interior Elevation. Pen and ink on paper by John McComb, Jr.

Gracie Mansion, at 88th Street, and City Hall, in lower Manhattan—early nineteenth-century New York edifices under construction at practically the same time—are today at either end of an axis on which the mayor's life revolves. Although the architect, John McComb, Jr., is credited with the prize-winning design of City Hall, Ezra Weeks, the probable architect-builder of Gracie Mansion, also contributed to its construction.

27

this country, trade ties were sought for, and gained, with leading New York merchants.

In May 1803, the cornerstone of New York City Hall was laid. Two months later, as yellow fever raged in downtown Manhattan, Gracie's country house became a retreat from the epidemic and a place where his business might be continued, as this excerpt of an August letter from Wolcott indicates:

Direct your vessels to stop in the Cove, below Hell Gate, south of Genl Stevens' house with directions to have your letters left at Mr. Gracie's house on the opposite side of the river. The hands will thereby be safe and some detention avoided.

War between France and Britain broke out this same year. Gracie, like most New York shippers, had strong business and personal attachments in each nation. Both Gouverneur Morris, as minister to France, and Rufus King, as minister to Great Britain, had loaned money to Lafayette in prison in France; Gracie, their friend and business associate, is reported to have done likewise.

In the interests of the partners, Gracie's ship, the *Virginia*, was sent on a speculative journey around the Cape of Good Hope to Madras and Calcutta where prized Spanish dollars were exchanged for Indian baled cottons. In April 1805, the partnership was dissolved even before the *Virginia* returned. Wolcott wrote to a Massachusetts merchant: "I have dissolved my partnership here, in consequence of an agreement with my friends which is entirely satisfactory to all of us." Besides European and Near Eastern enterprises, the partnership had included transactions as diverse as investments in sugar from the Barbados and saltpeter from Russia, sales of land in Ohio's Western Reserve, a sloop in the East River and stock for Yale College—a bow, no doubt to the five Connecticut partners. Although the firm that included Wolcott and Gracie ended, friendship and business relations between the two—as well as with the other partners—continued.

In early May of 1803 Gracie represented a group of Alexander Hamilton's friends in the auction of Hamilton Grange for the benefit of Elizabeth Schuyler Hamilton, the widow of their distinguished comrade killed the summer before in the duel with Aaron Burr on the dueling ground overlooking the Hudson at Weehawken. Gracie, acting for himself and the other friends and associates who had bought shares to aid the widow, purchased The Grange at auction for $30,000. They resold it to her for half that amount. Gracie and Mrs. Hamilton's English brother-in-law, John Barker Church, continued to oversee the property after the sale.

On September 29, 1804, Hamilton's widow had sought aid from

Gracie in another direction, as her son, Alexander Hamilton, Jr., eighteen years old and a Columbia graduate, was placed in the counting house of "Mr. Gracy and Wollcott." Hamilton was the agent, or supercargo, sent on the firm's ship bound for Cadiz, but Gracie's fellow merchant, John Pintard, observed that the young man had "wasted the consignment to considerable amount," and "returned blemished as to probity and character."

In 1802 and 1803 the three oldest Gracie children were in their low to mid-teens and the two youngest, Robert and Esther, were infants. In these years, therefore, Gracie's large family was still living at home, his prosperity and prospects were on the rise, and he was already looking for property on which to build houses where his family might live in style in spacious quarters of its own.

Josiah Quincy, a young Bostonian who was the guest of honor at dinner in Gracie's country house in 1805, offered a description of the view:

A deep, broad, rapid stream glances with an arrowy fleetness by the shore, hurrying along every species of vessel which the extensive commerce of the country affords. The water broken by the rocks which lie in the midst of the current, presents a continued scene of turbulent waves, dashing, foaming and spending their force upon the rocks. The various courses every vessel has to shape, in order to escape from the dangers of the pass, present a constant change and novelty in this enchanting scene. The shores of Long-Island full of cultivated prospects and interspersed with elegant country-seats, bound the distant view.

At the same time, he noted "Wolcott's character of Gracie" as "one of the most excellent of the earth—actively liberal, intelligent, seeking and rejoicing in occasions to do good. Certainly, I have great reason to be grateful for his attention."

Quincy viewed with delight "the prospect from the summer house," which is likely to have been the prospect of Hell Gate thrice published in England. He "strolled about the splendid gardens," an indication that landscaping of the site kept pace with that of the country seats along the East River that were rising nearby.

The gardens were an interest that Gracie shared with Dr. David Hosack, one of four gentlemen invited as guests to the Quincy dinner. Besides Hosack and his host, the others present at the mansion house were Judge Nathaniel Pendleton, who had been Hamilton's second in his duel with Burr (Pendleton's daughter was to marry Esther Gracie's nephew, Moses Rogers' son); Oliver Wolcott, who arranged for the dinner and was Gracie's business associate and lifelong friend (his daughter, Elizabeth, was to marry William Gracie); and a Mr. Hopkins. (Susan Lyman concludes that this was

29

"York Island with a View of the seats of Mr. A. Gracie . . ."
From an original by William Birch, engraved and published in *Country Seats of The United States*, Philadelphia, 1808. *This delightful long-range view of upper Manhattan from Long Island shows Gracie Mansion close to the time that Archibald Gracie enlarged the house, adding a porch and a large wing onto its west side. To the left, next to the trellis, is the Cruger House, then owned by the widow of Nicholas Cruger. Between the Cruger and Gracie houses are buildings that may be intended to represent Archibald Gracie's stone stable (on the river just north of present 86th Street) and possibly John Jacob Astor's house (the small gable-ended building above the roof of the other structure). To the right of Gracie Mansion is the property purchased in 1807 by Nathaniel Prime. Beyond it, on the point, right of Horn's Hook, are buildings on William Rhinelander's land.*

First-floor plan of Gracie Mansion.
Pen-and-ink drawing by Robert Meadows, 1981. *The changes that occurred when the mansion was enlarged early in the nineteenth century may be seen by comparing this plan to the conjectural drawing of the floor plan of Gracie's original house. The exterior walls of the addition on the right (the large drawing room with the kitchen behind it) are much thicker than those of the original house. The dining room, upper left, was enlarged to encompass the eastern half of the old hall, while its western area was absorbed into the new north-south axis of the divided reception and stair hall.*

Samuel Miles Hopkins, husband of Esther Gracie's niece, Sarah Woolsey.)

The same year as Quincy's visit, the Gracies were still spending most of their time in Richard Varick's rented house on Broadway as construction of their two houses on Pearl Street went forward. One was a "large 3-story house with a yard running through to Bridge Street," at No. 1 Pearl Street: the other, at No. 3, also had a yard through to Bridge Street. Both were finished "in the best manner . . . replete with conveniences," and "Command a most extensive view of the bay."

Many years after the event, the redoubtable May King Van Rensselaer, a Gracie granddaughter (who figures prominently in the mansion's early twentieth-century history), described an evening party there in May 1804. It was attended by friends, many of them coming from the city six miles away. Tea and coffee were served from a large silver service and plum cake was passed "in a great silver cake basket." Guests entertained themselves at cards, dancing and with informal music at the pianoforte. On this occasion, after several young guests had performed, Gracie brought forth a stranger for a song. As rumors of his success as a poet and his friendship with the Prince of Wales circled the room, he recited rather than sang several odes to Anacreon.

One of the guests, John Van Buren, son of the president, who knew the singer from having crossed swords with him on an earlier occasion, evened a score by loudly asking, "Who is the queer little man who seems to have left his voice under a pillow?" The story may be apocryphal, but the "queer little man" reciting his own work was Irish musician and poet Thomas Moore, the author of "The Harp That Once Through Tara's Halls," "Believe Me If All Those Endearing Young Charms," and "The Last Rose of Summer."

Archibald Gracie made the addition to the house that brought it to almost its present appearance sometime between 1802 and 1804. The evidence for the addition lies in a print issued in 1808 of Archibald Gracie's country seat at Hell Gate. It is a long-range view from Long Island of the enlarged house with the central hall axis and front door—formerly facing directly on the river—now moved so that the entrance faced the inlet at the north boundary of Horn's Hook.

A porch is visible across the east and north sides of the house. Modern investigation reveals that the walls of the addition to the house are considerably thicker than the original ones. Their joining—to the right under the front steps—shows carefully fitted stone foundations in the old area, and sturdy but less artful foundations abutting it in the new addition.

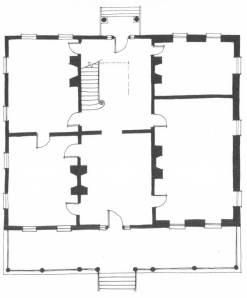

31

(above)

"The Seat of Archibald Gracie Esq. of Hurl Gate near Niew York, taken from the river."

Watercolor attributed to a student of Archibald Robertson, ca. 1810.

Better than any other, this unlocated drawing of Archibald Gracie's mansion shows the relation between the house and the land and river at Horn's Hook. The open porch (later enclosed with a rail) encircles the side of the house on the river and extends across the entrance facade. As first built, the front entrance faced the river but, early in the eighteenth century, Gracie nearly doubled the size of the house, adding on a wing to the west and moving the front entrance to the position seen here, its present conformation.

(top right)

Hell Gate.

Colored aquatint published by Moses Thomas, engraved by John Hill from a drawing by Joshua Shaw, in *Picturesque Views of American Scenery*, Philadelphia, 1819.

The view, from the north side of the inlet at Horn's Hook, shows the elegant fence that circled Archibald Gracie's property, rising from the stone wall that held the steep embankment at river's edge. The gate leads to steps down to a little bathing pavilion on the inlet. At center right is Mill Rock with the blockhouse built on it as part of the fortification of Long Island Sound, the East River access to New York during the War of 1812.

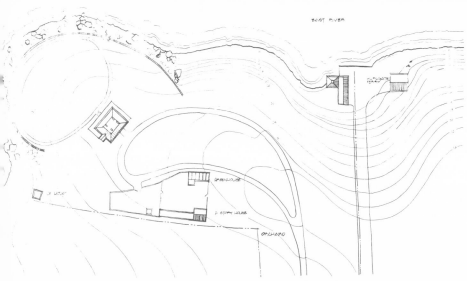

(left)

The Site–1810.
Pen-and-ink rendering by Philip N.
Winslow, Landscape Architect,
September 1981.
*Imprinted upon the Horn's Hook property of
Archibald Gracie in this conjectural view are
the improvements and additions that Gracie
made to the house and land early in the
nineteenth century. The house is enlarged to
almost its present conformation. The sea wall
and fence are shown around the point of land
overlooking Hell Gate, as is the promenade
that circled the lawn. Icehouse, orchard, two-
story house, greenhouse and stone stable—all
mentioned in contemporary descriptions of the
property—are in place, as is the little pleasure
house and bathing pavilion, incorporated into
the stone wall at river's edge.*

View of New York from East River.
Watercolor by an unidentified artist,
ca. 1810.
*In this view from the northern tip of today's
Roosevelt Island, the west bank of the East
River is seen with the Cruger House at the
level of present-day 85th Street. At center
right, on the shore north of the walk and drive
to the river, is Archibald Gracie's stone stable,
built at about this time. Gracie Mansion in
its completed state is at the right of the stable.
The wall of placed river rock and cut stone
that surrounded the mansion in Gracie's time
is seen along the East River shore at Horn's
Hook.*

The 1808 view, by Thomas Birch, locates Gracie's country seat in relation to its neighbors to the south and west. A near view by a pupil of Archibald Robertson (another Scots artist with the same name as the topographical draftsman and engineer who recorded the Walton house and its destruction) was drawn at about the same time. It shows the enlarged house in close-up, and the graceful Chinese Chippendale railings at the eave line and above the porch. The mansion, its remarkable trees and the lawn sloping down to a carefully constructed sea wall rising above huge river rocks are delineated. A picket fence with decorative urn finials encloses the property and the steps leading down to an elegant little bathhouse on the inlet. In *Picturesque Views of American Scenery*, published in Philadelphia in 1819, the view from this point was illustrated and described again:

The annexed view was taken from the grounds of Mr. Gracie {foot of 88th Street}, which commands one of the finest prospects on the East River . . .
The building on the rock to the right hand of the picture, is a fort or block-house {Mill Rock and Fort}. The interest of the scene is continually varying, in consequence of the sunken rocks which abound in this spot, and the water on different appearance on the return of the tide from that which it exhibits at its setting in. At some periods it boils up and foams, while its tremendous roaring can be heard at a great distance; and the frequent whirlpools render navigation dangerous, unless with skilful pilots . . .

An astute and informed observer, Dr. Samuel Latham Mitchill, physician, scientist and botanist, in writing the city's first guidebook, *Picture of New York*, in 1807, said of the same view:

At a convenient time of tide, it is very agreeable to see vessels pass through this place of intricate navigation. It is by no means uncommon to see ships and even sloops laying bilged on the reefs, notwithstanding all the care and skill of the navigators. It is computed that during the mild season of the year, between five and six hundred sail of vessels go through this passage weekly. And they are not merely coasting craft but brigs and ships of large size.

Mitchill went on to describe what could only be the completed structure as "The present elegant Mansion" and its "appurtenances." With the new addition, the interior was reorganized so that the old hall was incorporated into a dining room on the river side; the west side became part of a new double hall, created from the original one and the two rooms that adjoined it. The heavy new walls enclosed a formal drawing room, with a fireplace and a new small parlor on the southwest corner of the first floor. Upstairs, there were five bedchambers and, on the third floor, a large unfinished attic open to the rafters. Kitchen and service quarters were probably in the basement.

Some further improvements and additions to the house were completed about 1810 when a large watercolor by an unknown artist was painted. The view is west and north from the upriver tip of Blackwell's (now Roosevelt) Island, and the nearest structure is the Cruger country seat on the river at about 85th Street. Small fishing and sailboats ply the river, and fishermen from shore and afloat try their luck in waters teeming with fish. Favored food for feasting, turtles and oysters abounded here, especially in the coves and inlets on the shores of the river. A little to the right of the center of the painting, Archibald Gracie's great stone stable is already in place at the foot of 86th Street, just north of the Hurlgate Ferry, established in 1802. (Invisible in this view is the landing where ferryman Jacob McKeag and his family lived.) The completed mansion stands at Horn's Hook, surrounded by the noble trees mentioned in most descriptions. The river wall has, as part of it, the small turreted pleasure house overlooking the water.

South of the mansion, parallel to present East End Avenue at about 87th Street, was "a little rustic farmhouse with its fences burdened by wild grape" and behind it a greenhouse and barnyard. Farther south, on the reversed L which was the access to the Hurlgate Ferry road, was an orchard.

At the start of Jefferson's second term as President in 1805, one of Gracie's many charitable contributions to his adopted city began as he and others were empowered by the State Legislature "to establish a Free School in the City of New York for the education of such poor children as do not belong to or are not provided for by any religious society." Gracie became one of 13 original trustees of the school. That same year Gracie was named as a founding director of the New York branch of The Bank of the United States, a post he held until 1811, when the bank's charter expired.

Early in 1806, Gracie met the Scots merchant David Parish, sent to New York to effect a complicated exchange of Mexican silver to pay the terms of a Spanish treaty made between Spain's Charles IV and Napoleon. In this, the international high jinks called the Spanish Affair, a French banking house was given royal licenses and the exclusive right to pay the debt through Mexico, Spain's colony. Although at war with England, the French enlisted the aid of the English branch of Hope & Company and of John Irving of Reid, Irving & Company. (Gracie already had ties with both companies.)

Parish came to New York as Hope & Company's agent and was assigned office space in Gracie's counting house. Miss Lyman concludes that this arrangement took place as a direct result of Gracie's friendship with Rufus King and Gouverneur Morris, the former American ambassadors to France and Great Britain respectively.

Within a month the complicated scheme to transfer gold and silver to a North American port by way of Vera Cruz was arranged. New Orleans, a comparatively short run across the Gulf of Mexico, offered the nearest available harbor in the move to bypass British warships. The English vessels, patrolling Atlantic and Caribbean waters, were set to pounce on French or Spanish vessels, or on neutral American ships suspected of trading with the enemy or of having British subjects among their crews.

Gracie, accustomed to complicated scheduling of long-term merchant-ship voyages to international ports, was sought out to build and employ swift 100-ton, one- or two-masted pilot boats in the service between Vera Cruz and New Orleans. There, Parish's agent, Vincent Nolte, would forward the money or convert it into salable goods. (Nolte is the life model for Anthony Adverse in the historical novel of the same name by Hervey Allen in which Parish appears as himself.) The business was risky, and Parish in a February 1806 letter to Gracie urges him to warn the pilot boat captains "to speak nothing and run away from every sail you see on the ocean." Among the first of the pilot boats to make the run was Gracie's schooner, *Aspasia*, sent by Nolte to Vera Cruz loaded with German linen. On her return to New Orleans she bore a different cargo of more than $50,000 in Mexican specie.

Parish, meanwhile, wrote to Hope & Company in London, giving it information which, presumably, it already had,

Archibald Gracie enjoying excellent credit and generally respected for his honorable and upright principles: he is most sincerely and devotedly attached to the house and being at the same time a very discreet man, I think fully deserves to be your confidential man in this place.

The Spanish Affair was made to appear as private business between private companies. As far as Gracie was concerned, he involved not only himself and his New York company but also Gracie, Anderson and Co. in Petersburg. To maintain the cloak of secrecy over the important merchants and head of state who were participants, Parish adopted an identifying code in his papers: Gracie becoming *WW* and Napoleon Bonaparte, *qq*.

Between March 1806 and August 1807 Gracie had at least six pilot
boats intermittently working in this international scheme, including
the *Hettie*, named for his wife, and the newest one, especially built for
the trade, named *Hamilton* for his deceased friend. On the return
from Vera Cruz the boats customarily carried up to $150,000 in
specie, silver or gold. Examples of Gracie's continuing association
with Wolcott are the latter's accounts for four of the profitable
voyages.

Lyman sums up the bizarre finale of this international affair:

*England, the enemy of France and Spain, not only winked at the whole
performance but eventually profited by it. She was desperately in need of . . .
silver for the East India trade, and late in the spring of 1807 she was
permitted to send four frigates to Vera Cruz and bring out a total of
$14,000,000. Gracie's* Champlin *helped ferry the money from shore to ship.
After everyone had cooperated in this project, the various nations resumed
blockading. By July the affair came to a close, Parish reporting to Gouverneur
Morris: "My Dollar boats are all arrived without having been boarded by any
of the English cruizers—I have extracted since I left you last November upwards
of 5 millions of Dollars and you may easily conceive that my feelings are very
much justified to have been able to operate to such an extent without meeting
with any losses whatsoever." Soon afterwards, Parish returned to Europe,
Archibald disposed of the last of his pilot boats, and counted his gains while,
throughout the United States, discussion intensified on the pros and cons of a
possible embargo.*

In about 1806 the family—including Mrs. Gracie's 83-year-old
mother—moved into its new house at No. 1 Pearl Street. Next door,
at No. 3, lived Elizabeth and David Lambert, Esther Gracie's sister
and brother-in-law. The move to their own downtown residence after
11 years of renting the Broadway house of Richard Varick took place
at a time when the fortunes of all New York merchants were on the
rise. Among them, Gracie was almost the most favored. The
following year, 1807, which saw Robert Fulton's *Clermont* successfully
navigating the Hudson River, was also the peak export year in the
city's history to that date, with the port doing more than 26 million
in business.

But for most merchant shippers, December 1807 to the spring of
1809 were black times as President Jefferson placed an embargo on all
trade. In November 1806, Napoleon had issued his Berlin decree
threatening seizure of any ship that stopped in England. Britain's
Orders in Council that followed forbade any neutral to trade with
France. In retaliation, Napoleon's Milan Decree of November 1807
declared that any ship that complied with British demands was a

lawful prize. In this web of strictures on shipping issued by the warring nations before a United States embargo was imposed, Gracie lost the cargoes of two large vessels, the brig *Perseverance*, and the ship *Mary*. These and his other grave losses in this period were set at one million dollars, losses that began his financial ruin and later led to his claims on the French and English governments.

Jefferson's Embargo Act was to take effect in late December 1807 and as unofficial word reached New York on Christmas Eve, Lyman notes that

the cold dawn of Christmas Day was marked by an extraordinary exodus as alert captains of dozens of sailing ships headed out to sea. As it was, over five hundred boats were stranded in this one port alone.
The situation was the same everywhere, and the ditty printed in the Newburyport paper was as applicable to Yorkers as to Massachusetts men.
"Our ships all in motion once whitened the ocean
They sailed and returned with a cargo
Now doomed to decay, they have fallen a prey
To Jefferson, worms and embargo."

In 1808, although no ships moved along the South Street waterfront, Gracie began construction of a new counting house at No. 24 Whitehall Street at the far end of the block on which he lived. The building extended 80 feet along Bridge Street; stables and a coach house took up an additional 50 feet. By 1810, when it was complete, Gracie and Company had already become Archibald Gracie and Son, the name changed when William, at 21, joined the firm. In the year that the new counting house opened, Charles King, son of Rufus King, educated at Harrow, and initiated into commerce at London's Hope & Company offices, married Eliza, Archibald Gracie's oldest daughter, and also became a member of the firm, now renamed Archibald Gracie and Sons. At about the same time, Gracie added three new East River built vessels to his fleet, the *Canton*, *Oronoko* and *Eliza Gracie*.

The family had no sooner moved into their new downtown house than Gracie began plans for the largest and grandest of his dwellings, on property west of No. 1 Pearl Street that included the entire frontage on State Street between Pearl and Bridge Streets. The land, offered to Gracie by Governor Daniel Tompkins, was purchased from the State. The plot, at Broadway and State Street, bordered on the gardens of Government House, erected in 1790 and planned as the official home for the president when New York was the nation's capital. Construction of Gracie's latest house on a grand scale was not completed until 1812.

Mill Rock and Hell Gate from Fort Stevens.
Watercolor rendering by John Joseph Holland (1776–1820).
This view, taken from Fort Stevens on Hallett's Point, L.I., depicts the east shore of Manhattan and the salt meadow near the present 96th Street, as well as the blockhouse on Mill Rock, in the middle of the river. This plan is from a collection of 33 maps, plans and views of the fortifications constructed on Manhattan Island during the war of 1812, originally bound with the Report on the Defence of the City of New York . . . *by J.G. Swift, Brig. Gen., Chief Engineer of the United States, 1814.*

The Land at Horn's Hook.
Plate 12 in Sackersdorf's *Blue Book, Maps of Farms,* 1815.
The maps of New York farms, published in 1868, shows Horn's Hook at far right center and the relation between Archibald Gracie's country seat and the surrounding properties. The New York street grid, developed in 1807, but not implemented in this area until well past mid-century, shows 86th Street at the Hell Gate Ferry landing (here shown as a spur at the southeast corner of Gracie's land) and Avenue B cutting into its west boundary. The foot of the reversed L leading to Hell Gate Ferry Road (the meandering east-west double line) was Gracie's right of way.

In 1812, Lyman recounts,

Even as the United States declared war on England on June 11, 1812, three Gracie ships, with the America *in the lead, were on the high seas returning from grain deliveries in Portugal. George Coggleshall, captain of the* America, *successfully eluded British cruisers off Sandy Hook to reach New York safely, but the others, the* Eliza Gracie *and* Oronoko *were captured: the former burned at sea and the latter taken to Halifax.*

Under licenses issued by the British Privy Council, Gracie continued to send out grain shipments until 1813 when his *Protectress* and *Rolla* were captured and sent to British ports.

In the first year of the War of 1812 some military authorities saw the water route through Long Island Sound and Hell Gate as the most vulnerable point for British attack. Fortifications sprang up at Mill Rock and in a string of small posts built across Manhattan. Fort Stevens was erected at Hallett's Point and 12 guns were mounted there. In May the Common Council of New York ordered "that a corps of 120 cartmen be enlisted at $1.50 a day" to move the 40 pieces of heavy artillery from the United States Arsenal on Bloomingdale Road. Soon after, some of these cannon were removed to earthworks at Gracie's Point to guard the passage of Hell Gate.

Despite the fears of some concerning the Horn's Hook site, the entire Gracie family spent the summer of 1812 at the country seat. Among those summering at the mansion were Eliza and Charles King with their 18-month-old daughter, Eliza; in July, their second daughter was born there. Washington Irving spent that summer "only a ten minute walk away" from Gracie Mansion. Early in 1813, he wrote Henry Brevoort that the Gracies' country seat "was one of my strongholds last summer . . . It is a charming warm-hearted family and the old gentleman has the soul of a prince."

In June 1812, as the Bank of New York was chartered, Philip Hone and Gracie were among the 18 founding directors as Oliver Wolcott became its first president. In the biography of his father, prepared by his namesake in 1853, Archibald Gracie, Jr., maintained that "after the declaration of war Mr. Gracie thought seriously of retiring from these active pursuits, and of engaging in the business of banking." As early as 1811 he began the long and discouraging attempt to recoup the losses of cargo and ships from both the British and French governments as claims were presented in Paris for the loss of the cargoes of the *Mary* and the *Perseverance* valued at 1,210,923 francs. There was an official acknowledgment of the claim but no settlement.

Late in the year Gracie was one of the planners of a huge ceremonial

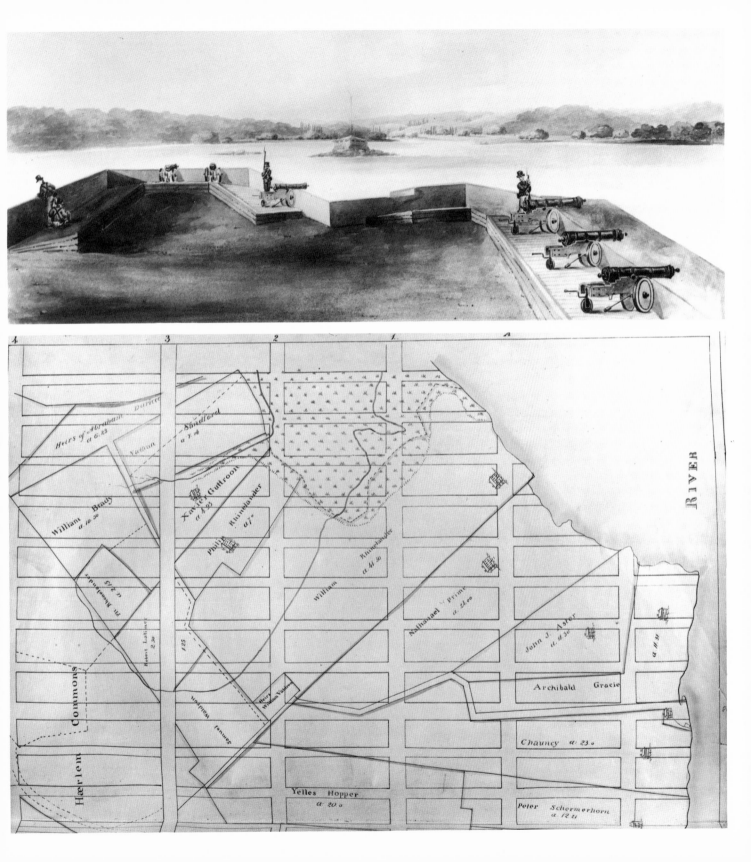

dinner held on December 29, 1812 at City Hotel, which had been transformed into a marine palace. There were miniature ships upon each table and a great mainsail furled behind the speaker's table. At the fourth toast, to "Our Navy," the mainsail was unfurled to reveal a transparent painting representing the three great naval victories won by the three honorees, Commodore Isaac Hull, Commodore Stephen Decatur and Captain Jacob Jones. (Hull's victory of the *Constitution* over the *Guerriere* must have given Gracie some satisfaction, for the *Guerriere* had been one of the wolf pack that had captured the *Eliza Gracie* and the *Oronoko*.) Irving wrote his brother, "It was the most splendid entertainment of the kind I ever witnessed . . . I never in my life before felt the national feeling so strongly aroused."

Even as plans for celebration of the three great marine victories went forward, Decatur's *United States* and his prize, the *Wasp*, hard-won in battle in the Azores, lay off Gracie Mansion, "waiting," Miss Lyman tells us, "for favorable winds and tides to carry them through Hell Gate and down to the city." They made it on New Year's Day.

"The war has completely changed the face of things," Irving wrote in his *Journal* as New York was once more blockaded by the British fleet early in 1813. "You would scarcely recognize our old peaceful city. Nothing is Talked of but armies, navies, battles, etc." Some of the talking took place at Gracie Mansion, as Mayor De Witt Clinton, Rufus King, the *Evening Post*'s William Coleman and other "Friends of Peace" met to plan for a mass meeting downtown. Nothing came of the peacemaking attempts as British warships moved into the harbor.

The Gracie children continued the marriages that brought their father's business and social relations close. Early in 1813, James Gore King married Sarah Rogers Gracie in the new State Street house. Eliza and Charles King lived at No. 3 Pearl Street while No. 1 was vacant until July 1813, when William Gracie and his bride, Elizabeth Wolcott moved in following their marriage in Oliver Wolcott's house at No. 26 Pine Street. (Six years later Elizabeth was to die of apoplexy at the country seat, an event compressed in legend to their wedding night.)

In 1813 Charles King made an attempt at collecting the British debt and presented a claim for losses to the Privy Council for Trade; on July 9 the Council refused to recognize the claim. Early in July 1814, as British men-o'-war again appeared off Sandy Hook, the harbor was well protected; with two new forts—Castles Williams and Clinton—and 350 pieces of artillery ranged at the Battery and around the

Manhattan side of the harbor. Oliver Wolcott put out a call for volunteers for the raising of batteries at vulnerable Brooklyn Heights as citizens of all levels of society—including a band of 300 women—responded enthusiastically.

The war ended with the signing of the Treaty of Ghent by British and American representatives on Christmas Eve in 1814. On February 11 the news reached New York. Although candles appeared that evening in house windows along Broadway, State and adjoining streets, the chief celebration took place two weeks later, outdoing, Miss Lyman notes, anything produced before in "this ceremony-minded city." Thirty-three firework set pieces were fired off from a huge stage in the form of a Temple of Peace constructed in front of Government House. The fireworks and temple cost a whopping $10,000. Miss Lyman describes the celebration that involved many city and country friends— and the artisan who is likely to have provided furnishings for Gracie's many mansions:

City Hall was illuminated with thousands of wax candles that outlined the roof, windows, and doors with flickering light, while transparencies were installed in each window. These banners of translucent material, painted with appropriate patriotic scenes and lighted from behind with special candles, were the popular form of decoration used in public buildings, stores and private homes . . . Duncan Phyfe strung a long row of nineteen illuminated lamps across the street in front of his shop, each bearing the picture of one of Our Naval Heroes {and} of George Washington; John Jacob Astor transformed his front door way into a temple entrance and surmounted it with an American Eagle Letting Fall the Sword. Nathaniel Prime not only decorated his large house at One Broadway but invited between two and three hundred guests to a celebration party. Undoubtedly all the Gracies attended this affair at their neighbors'.

Archibald's own house had an illumination featuring a ship under full sail and, beneath it, the motto Amity and Commerce with the World.

Although the war had taken a heavy toll on Gracie, he continued to seek ways to secure the financial futures of his children. In 1815 James Gore King entered into a partnership with Gracie, his father-in-law, and with the Petersburg firm of Walker & Atkinson with whom Gracie had long had business relations. Rufus King, father-in-law of two Gracie daughters, was a helpful friend in both business and pleasure. In early November King described a breakfast—for men only—honoring Napoleon's brother, one of the mansion's most distinguished visitors in the early nineteenth century:

On Wednesday Mr. Gracie gave a Breakfast to the Count Survilliers, alias

Mrs. William Gracie (1795–1819).
Oil on canvas by John Trumbull, ca. 1815.
Elizabeth Stoughton Wolcott was the daughter of Oliver Wolcott, Jr., governor of Connecticut. She was married on July 2, 1813, to William Gracie, son of Archibald Gracie. Joseph H. Scoville, who knew both families, wrote in his Old Merchants of New York *that "Wolcott's beautiful daughter married . . . William Gracie. Never did a bridal couple enter into married life with more brilliant prospects of happiness." But on June 26, 1819,* The New York Evening Post *carried the notice of Mrs. Gracie's death and reported that the funeral would be held at Gracie Mansion. In 1803, a commercial establishment was formed by Wolcott, Archibald Gracie, James Watson, Moses Rogers (Gracie's brother-in-law) and William W. Woolsey as commission merchants and agents. While the firm, Oliver Wolcott and Company, remained in existence for only a brief time, Gracie and Wolcott continued their friendship and business association.*

*J.B. {Joseph Bonaparte}; The Count St. Jean D'Angely and 3 or 4 young
Frenchmen came with the great Personage,—John & James {King}, with 1 or
2 Gentlemen of the City were invited. I was also present—*
*. . . A day or two after the arrival of the Ct. S., he made a little excursion
in the neighborhood of the City, and strolled into Mr. Gracie's grounds. The
family invited him into the house without knowing who he was, in this way
Mr. G., John & James, who were at Mr. Gracie's, became known to the Ct.,
who preserves his incognito and declines entering into Society.*

Early in 1815 Charles King returned to England to renew his
campaign for settlement of Gracie claims in England and France.
Later that year, Eliza Gracie King and their three children joined him,
escorted on the journey by 19-year-old Archibald Gracie, Jr., and by
Dr. John Francis, first librarian of the New-York Historical Society
and, at mid-century, the author of a fine history of New York. On
this journey, however, his charge was Eliza King, who was frequently
in poor health. Washington Irving met the party in Liverpool at mid-
September.
Irving had already written home his opinion of Eliza's husband,
"Charles is exactly what an American should be abroad—frank, manly
and unaffected in his sentiments toward other nations, but most
loyally attached to his own." Soon after welcoming Gracie's daughter
and her children, the American author wrote of the meeting in
another letter:

*The children are in fine health and spirits . . . Little Eliza is as wild as an
Indian and delighted with everything around her. Little Hettie is a beautiful
creature and the Boy {Rufus} a Noble Animal. I never saw a Nobler child
. . . The children have absolutely astonished the people at the hotel. You know
the great decorum of the English and the system of quiet and reserve by which
their children are brought up to behave like little men and women—whereas
the little Kings who are full of spirits and health, are just as noisy and
frolicksome as if out at Hell Gate—and racket about the hotel just as they
would at Papa Gracie's in State Street. I was infinitely amused with their
rantipole gambols—the little creatures are like birds let loose from a cage. Eliza
King showed me, with great pride, a certificate of good behavior of herself and
Hettie, during the voyage, signed by the passengers.*

After the King family reunion, they traveled to Scotland, to
Archibald Gracie's birthplace in Dumfries. His son-in-law was made a
freeman of the town and in return treated the community to a
"harangue"—dinner and speeches, aided by toasts in fine claret.
Archibald Gracie's gathering business troubles are revealed in a letter
to King written early in 1816: "From present prospects I think

ships will be a bad property especially to those who cannot find employment for them. Freights have not been so low for many years as at present."

In the fall of 1817, Gracie, "of the City of New York Merchant, being about to depart upon a voyage to Europe," made his will. The voyage was another attempt toward recovering his large English and French claims.

Joseph A. Scoville, who had been a youthful clerk in Gracie's counting rooms, relates, in his many-volumed account of New York merchants of the nineteenth century, the problems that arose in his mentor's absence from the city:

I have frequently alluded to the immense business the house did for years. Their operations were enormous. In the War of 1812, their losses were very heavy. Afterwards old Mr. Gracie went to Europe, leaving the business to be carried on by his son, William Gracie, and his son-in-law, Charles King, who formed the "Sons" of the firm. He left them with full power-of-attorney to act for him, and, if need be, to sell his real estate. While the old gentleman was abroad, the sons went into enormous cotton speculations and lost immensely. They borrowed $100,000 of the Bank of New York. I think Rufus King was security. At any rate, the sons used the power-of-attorney to convey to old Mr. King the real estate of Mr. Gracie comprising in it the country seat at Gracie's Point.

Although Gracie remained in Europe until June 1819 he was unsuccessful in settling the claims against either government. Further disappointment awaited, as he returned to find that business at home had taken a disastrous turn.

William Gracie and Charles King had borrowed $215,000 from their uptown and downtown neighbor, Nathaniel Prime, giving in return promissory notes for $40,000 and insurance policies on the East Indian bound ship *Braganza* and half her cargo. A further loan, $100,000 of the total, was advanced just before Gracie's return. All of the company's "every part and portion of each of our houses stores messuages land and tenements" were sold to Rufus King to hold in security for this latest loan from Prime.

Within two weeks of his return, Gracie signed over to King a quit claim for all his property, although he continued to occupy the entailed houses, stores, warehouses and offices. In 1820 as both his business and the value of his property declined (the estimate of his wealth that year was $20,000, one third of what it had been five years earlier), Gracie continued to press his claims against England and France. Both Rufus King and Oliver Wolcott, then Governor of Connecticut, wrote to John Quincy Adams on their friend's behalf.

Wolcott pursued the matter as late as November 1823, when he once more pressed for settlement of the debts owed Gracie in a second letter to Adams on the subject:

During a recent visit from my highly estimable friend Archibald Gracie Esq. of New York, I have been made particularly acquainted with the circumstances by which this gentleman has been divested of an ample estate, the accumulations of a life of intelligent and active industry. I find it to be clearly demonstrable that his great losses are not to be attributed to the fluctuations of markets or any of the inevitable accidents which attend extensive commercial enterprizes, but solely to the perfidy and injustice of the British and French governments.

No man ever merited by his virtues the possession of wealth in a higher degree, no man has been more distinguished by every act of benevolence and generosity which he had the ability to perform and no misfortunes have excited more sincere and undissembled regrets among all classes of society than those which have marked the uniform career of Mr. Gracie. He entertains an opinion in which I concur, that he owes it to his character, the interests of his family and friends, and the cause of justice, to persevere in his exertions to obtain redress.

In late April, the advertisement for sale of all Gracie and Sons' property appeared, with Archibald Gracie's "unrivalled" country seat heading the list. Ezra Weeks, the most likely builder of Gracie Mansion, acted as agent for the sale of the properties. On May 5, 1823, the firm of Archibald Gracie and Sons was dissolved.

Several years before, Archibald Gracie had settled his sister-in-law and her husband in his then new house at No. 3 Pearl Street. Now the favor was returned as the Gracie family moved from No. 15 State Street to No. 14 Bond Street, to a house owned by David Lambert. Living with their parents were William Gracie, whose wife, Elizabeth Wolcott, had died at Gracie Mansion four years before, and Esther and David Gracie, the two youngest children. Lambert had built three "Marble Houses" on Bond Street, then in the upper part of the city, that were first advertised in the *New York Evening Post* two weeks before the sale of the Gracie property.

Archibald Gracie continued to seek redress for his French claims, and while President John Quincy Adams held that "the claims of Mr. Gracie upon the French Government are founded in strict justice," and noted that he would pursue the amounts to which Gracie was entitled, recognizing "his sufferings and his wrongs," Adams did not inform him further. Gracie continued his campaign, preparing memorials of his French claims for each member of Congress. While the French claims were not settled in the merchant's lifetime, British claims were. The claims of the defunct New York company were assigned to the English firm of King and Gracie which was granted 35 percent of the total debt or £21,000 sterling. By 1828 payment was complete.

Gracie's associates in St. Andrew's Society, citing their president's "usefulness," and wishing to provide "an asylum for his declining years," established The Atlantic Insurance Company with Gracie as its head. Although capitalized with $500,000, the company, in Miss Lyman's words, "got off to a poor start and Archibald soon pulled out," although the company did provide one social benefit to Gracie in being one of nine organizations to underwrite Lafayette's triumphal return to America in 1824.

The Erie Canal, completed late in 1825, brought unequaled prosperity to most New York merchants, but not to Archibald Gracie. Two personal tragedies added to the already heavy load of his business failure as Eliza Gracie King died in Cuba on a trip planned by her husband to aid her health. Four months later David Lambert was attacked by a street gang, the Spring Street Fencibles, and was killed. The marble houses went on the market, and once more the family moved—this time to a house at No. 629 Broadway, Gracie's last home. He walked two or three miles each day, regularly visiting the three leading papers to get the evening news.

On April 11, 1829, Gracie died of erysipelas—an acute, painful and inflammatory skin disease sometimes called St. Anthony's Fire. He was first buried in St. Thomas' Churchyard on Broadway, but today he rests in the Gracie plot in Woodlawn, surrounded by more than 20 of his relations.

The tributes were, says Lyman, many and all equally laudatory, but instead of quoting from the papers, let one of his contemporaries, John Pintard, speak of him:

"This afternoon," he wrote his daughter on April 13, 1829, "I am to attend the funeral of Archibald Gracie . . . once the most respectable merchant in this city, of unbounded hospitality and munificence, a subscriber to every religious and beneficent institution, esteemed and beloved above every citizen of his time. The French and British spoliations broke down his once princely establishment which depressed his spirits and eventually shortened his days."

The Foulkes and Wheatons at Gracie Mansion, 1828–1896

In the spring of 1823, just a little more than two weeks after the firm of Archibald Gracie and Sons was dissolved, Joseph Foulke, another merchant shipper, bought Gracie Mansion. While there is no record of bankruptcy proceedings in the dissolution of Gracie's firm, it was Rufus King, friend, business partner and the father-in-law of two Gracie daughters, who was trustee of Gracie's property and who sold the land to Foulke.

The country seat at Hell Gate had been advertised in the three New York newspapers in late April and early May. The parcel included the mansion, identified as "a very large double house," with "greenhouse, stables, coach and other outhouses complete, and about eleven acres of land, the whole in very fine order. The unrivaled beauty of this situation needs no description."

Foulke, born in Piscataway, New Jersey in 1769, established a profitable West Indian trade early in life, principally between New York and the island of Curaçao. In 1800, at the age of 31, Foulke married 15-year-old Charlotte Brion, daughter of Pierre Louis Brion, a rich merchant and member of the Curaçao Council of State. For a little more than 15 years after the marriage, the couple lived on the island, although Foulke made frequent business trips to New York. On April 1, 1805, for example, he became a Mason in Curaçao. Two months later he affiliated himself with New York's Hiram Masonic Lodge.

The couple's eighth child was born on Curaçao in 1816; when the ninth and next-to-last child was born in 1818, the family was already living in New York. In the directory of that year an office is listed for Joseph Foulke at No. 470 Broadway. The following year his business was located along the waterfront, at No. 155 South Street, with a residence at No. 12 Dey Street. By 1820 the family had moved to No. 81 Chambers Street, as Foulke's personal worth was set at $15,000. Early in the administration of John Quincy Adams, the large family used Gracie Mansion only as a summer residence; the directory of 1825 to 1826, for instance, lists a house at No. 69 Franklin Street. Soon after this date, however, as the city's population went over 200,000, the Foulkes and their children (the youngest then about six years old) moved into the country house as a year-round residence.

The neighboring estates, like those of Nathaniel Prime, John Jacob Astor and Isaac Chauncey, were maintained and used by their original owners, their descendants, or new and equally affluent owners throughout the period that the Foulke family enjoyed their beautiful mansion on the land at Horn's Hook. But the onward march of the city's uptown growth continued, in the late summer and fall of 1832 spurred by an epidemic of cholera downtown. Commercial establishments, small tenements and rental units began to spring up at the land borders of the large country seats along the river.

Transportation often preceded development, and in 1833 the Harlem Railroad was extended to Yorkville along Park (then Fourth) Avenue; in 1835, Third Avenue was opened from 28th Street north to Harlem. Inflation, the result of President Jackson's removal of federal funds from the Bank of the United States, began in 1836. In 1837, as Samuel F. B. Morse continued to refine his newly invented telegraph in his laboratory at New York University, the panic of 1837, soon to affect most New Yorkers, began.

Foulke had become a director of the Hope Insurance Company at about the time of his purchase of Gracie Mansion. In 1839, following the panic, he was elected to the Board of Directors of City Bank. By 1842, his wealth had increased enormously, and his net worth in the periodic summation of *Wealth & Biography of the Wealthy Citizens of New York City* was placed at $300,000. Three years later, as he was described as "an English gentleman of the highest rank among our honorable merchants," it was noted that his three sons, Joseph, William and Theodore, had joined their father "in the West Indian importing business."

Despite this characterization of Foulke as an English gentleman, he maintained ties with the town of his birth and offered assistance when Piscataway Church was destroyed by a tornado in 1835. In August of the following year, the new church "was erected at the sole expense of Mr. Joseph Foulke of Harlegate near Near York, a native of Piscataway."

In his own neighborhood, Foulke opposed an 1837 recommendation to the Common Council for the opening of 86th Street between Eighth Avenue and the East River. The way, "between Third Avenue and the Hurlgate Ferry," was "narrow zigzag and inconvenient," and "almost impassable at certain seasons of the year." Despite the opposition of Foulke and some of his neighbors, it was decided to open the street. Work on the road continued a year, and when a hill north of the ferry was blasted, the old stone stable of Archibald Gracie was damaged slightly.

Two drawings of Hell Gate in 1841 and 1842 show the river inlet and the great houses west of Gracie Mansion. The docks and boathouses of the Prime House are seen head on and in side view in the drawings. Immediately north of the stable were two structures joined at an angle. They may have been boathouses or warehouses for loading and unloading cargo at the dock on Foulke property east of the stone stable.

Sixtieth Street at the East River.
Watercolor by an unidentified artist,
ca. 1820.

*The photograph of a lost watercolor, of the area
about a mile south of Gracie Mansion, shows
the ferry and East River landscape at the
location of the stone stable seen up present day
60th Street (the structure nearest the road, up
the hill to the right). Although the stable
survives as the Abigail Adams Smith House,
the main house, built for Colonel William
Stephens Smith in the eighteenth century, was
sold by him long before it vanished in a fire in
the spring of 1826. The Beekman House at
Rural Cove (63rd Street) appears just right of
center. Its greenhouse, where Major André was
imprisoned just before his execution as a
British spy, is thought to be similar to
Archibald Gracie's, up river at the level of the
present 87th Street.*

'Rural Cove" at 63rd Street and East River.

Watercolor by Ernest Finkernagel, 1851. *Proceeding up the East River from the present level of 60th Street, boat, yacht and ferry passengers saw a pastoral landscape on both shores. The heights on the Manhattan side were punctuated by a large number of country houses, most of them almost as grand as the Beekman House, the center of interest in this view.*

View of J. M. Dunlap's Hurlgate Ferry Hotel, foot of 86th Street and East River.

Color lithograph, published by James Baillie, ca. 1850.

The side-wheeler steamboat Knickerbocker *was in use on the East River for only a few years, from about 1846 to the early 1850s, and serves to date this lithograph of the Hurlgate Ferry Hotel at 86th Street and the East River. The stone stable built by Archibald Gracie is seen at center right; it was then in use as a storage warehouse for*

xchange or cargo between the land and the river. In this period the land south of Gracie Mansion was comparatively open. As the ferry to Astoria was moved north to 92nd Street in 1866, the land and ferry road fell into disuse and the stable was demolished.

(top right)
John Jacob Astor's Former Residence, 88th Street near East River.
Drawn by George Hayward for *Valentine's Manual*, 1864.
It was from this house, immediately west of Gracie's along the inlet north of Horn's Hook, that Washington Irving strolled to visit his neighbors in the summer of 1812 when he wrote Astoria; *the site on Long Island that gave him his title is seen immediately across the East River from Gracie Mansion, clearly visible from its lawn.*

(bottom right)
Hell Gate from 60th Street.
Pen and ink on paper by Eliza Greatorex, 1869.
This northeasterly view shows the west bank of the East River at about the point of the ferry landing at 61st Street. Hell Gate and the Queens side of the river are at far right. "Rural Cove," the Beekman Mansion at 63rd Street, is seen at the left. Lydia Beekman, who married Joseph Foulke's son, lived at "Rural Cove" during her childhood.

53

Noah Wheaton.
Photograph by an unidentified
photographer, ca. 1870.
The Wheatons were the third family to live at Gracie Mansion, occupying the house from 1857 to 1896. Wheaton, born in Hartford in 1808, began life as a cabinetmaker and builder, although an extant letter addressed to him in Hartford identifies him as an architect. In New York he made numerous changes and improvements in the mansion and surrounding grounds, while conducting a business in millwork, window blinds and other builders' supplies from a number of downtown locations.

Although the Foulkes lived at Gracie Mansion year round for almost 27 years, maps and personal recollections of the "unrivalled beauty" of the location at Horn's Hook most frequently identify the spot and recall its use and appearance in the years that Archibald Gracie lived there.

The specter of financial ruin, appearing in different guises to haunt the first and the last of the families who lived in the mansion in the nineteenth century—the Gracies and the Wheatons—became a recurring apparition, rarely leaving the house from 1857, the year of a panic less severe than the one of twenty years before, and 1884. In the latter year, Jane Wheaton, then in her late thirties, and the youngest child of Noah Wheaton, married former City Councilman Hamlin Babcock. In 1885, her husband took over financial responsibility and nominal ownership of the mansion. From then until 1896, when the Wheatons left, they enjoyed comparative freedom from financial woes.

In the winter of 1890, Noah Wheaton, then 82 years old, appeared before the New York City Commissioners of Estimate, who had continued hearings since 1888 to determine the owners of 36 parcels of land between Avenue B (East End Avenue) and the East River, and from 86th Street north to the Harlem and East Rivers at 90th Street. While ownership of the lots south of Gracie Mansion was fairly clear, the legal possessor or possessors of the Gracie Mansion site and the water lots that surrounded it to the north and east were far from easy to identify.

Wheaton testified before the commissioners that he had lived in the house for 32 years without interruption. As the hearings dragged on, his reply to a direct question concerning his view of ownership elicited a response neither evasive nor confused in the light of what is known of the history of the house. He said, "I can't answer that question. It is difficult to solve. I once owned it."

In 1854 Noah Wheaton first arrived in New York and rented a store at No. 32 Canal Street (between Broadway and Elm) as the location for his business in window blinds. The following year he rented a second shop at No. 113 Wall Street, near the East River between South and Front Streets. By then he and his family were living in New York at No. 68 West 31st Street. The following year they moved to No. 118 12th Street, a location more convenient to the shop than the 31st Street one.

For several years before his move to New York, entries in the Hartford Directory identify Wheaton as a house builder. Late in life, Wheaton observed that he had built "almost all kinds of houses." There is no direct evidence of his following this trade in New York, although the

Hell Gate from Great Barn Island.
Drawn and engraved by Archibald L.
Dick; printed by A. King, after 1833.
Astoria is seen at left, with the northern tip of
Roosevelt Island near the twin smokestacks of
the walking-beam steamboat and with
Manhattan at the right. Several homes are
visible on the East River shore, beginning with
the Hell Gate Tavern at the foot of 86th
Street. Gracie Mansion is seen between the
lines of the sailing ship on the left. The Prime
Mansion is near the right mast of the grounded
vessel.

***Hell Gate from Astoria, Long Island,
New York, 1841.***
Pencil on paper by an unidentified artist,
1841.
*The Prime Mansion and docks, near the foot of
90th Street, appear in the distance of a view
from the Long Island shore.*

Hellgate, 1842.
Photograph of a lost drawing by an
unidentified artist.
*This view from the Astoria, Long Island
shows the Prime, Rhinelander and Paulding
houses located just north of Gracie Mansion on
the west bank of the East River.*

millwork that he stocked at his stores might indicate that his early training as a joiner was being usefully applied.

Wheaton was born at North Branford, along the Connecticut River, in 1808. In 1834 he married Amelia Ball of New Haven. In 1849, the youngest of his four daughters, Alice Hermione, was born in Hartford. In 1853 his oldest child, seven-year-old Ellen Wheaton, died there.

That same year, the sons and executors of Joseph Foulke had subdivided the land that had once been Archibald Gracie's into city lots, and early in the spring of 1857, shortly after James Buchanan was inaugurated as fifteenth president, Noah Wheaton purchased the house and the 12 lots running from 88th to 89th Streets. The lots were in the center of the block, west to east, from Avenue B (East End Avenue) to the East River. It was a curious parcel. The eight lots contiguous to Avenue B were omitted, as were the seven steep and rocky water lots immediately bordering the East River. The house, set at an angle at the southwest corner of the lots, projected several feet into the allowance for 88th Street.

The price for this plot was $25,000 with Wheaton making the agreement to purchase with builder John Bunting and his wife Evalina. The Buntings lived downtown; in all likelihood they had bought the house and land only as an investment, having accepted a mortgage on an intervening sale of the property. These owners defaulted in 1855, and the Buntings, in reclaiming their house and lots, set into motion a series of liens, mortgages, defaults, understandings and misunderstandings that continued to resonate through the 39 years that the Wheatons, their children, sons-in-law and grandchildren occupied Gracie Mansion.

At the time of purchase Noah Wheaton seems to have arranged two mortgages. One was with the Great Western Insurance Company; the other was an agreement with the Buntings similar to the one they had with the defaulting owners of 1855. As soon as he bought the house, its latest owner set about improving the property. His first step was to acquire from the Crosby Street saloon keeper, William Niblo, the narrow water lot on the north side of Horn's Hook between the East River inlet and the mapped extension of 89th Street. Lot number 108 was subject to a mortgage held by Niblo, who owned other property within the former Gracie holdings—the lots immediately south of the mansion between 87th and 88th Streets, running from mid-block east to the river. A year and a half after his purchase of the water lot, Wheaton acquired from the city—for one dollar—the right to the underwater land north of lot 108.

As Wheaton started repair and alteration of the interior of the

mansion, he began construction of a large two-story brick stable near
the house. The Dripps maps published in 1864 cover the entire city
in a single volume, and the scale is, therefore, quite small. In the plan
of the area in that volume, the holdings of Nathaniel Prime, John
Jacob Astor and Archibald Gracie are outlined. Within the Gracie
plot, William Niblo and Theodore Foulke's lands in the 87th to 88th
Street grid are indicated. In the block between 88th and 89th Streets
only the house and the icehouse (off Wheaton's property, on the
northwest corner of the block) are sketched. The stable is mapped for
the first time in the real-estate and insurance atlas for 1870. It is
located directly on the Wheatons' west property line and is set
about 100 feet from the entrance to the enclosed porch containing
service stairs to the second floor and leading into the kitchen of the
mansion.

One of two tiny structures along the shoreline in this map conforms
to a description of the area recalling the appearance of the property
and surrounding water lots when the Wheaton girls were young:

*I spent many happy hours with the Wheatons who lived there. {The house} of
course ran to the water's edge. All along the edge was built a wall of loose
stones piled up carefully to a height of about ten feet. You perhaps remember the
little summer house that used to be located on that wall. Back of this summer
house some fifty feet and a little to the west was a root cellar and in this were
several cannonballs about six inches in diameter that Mr. Wheaton told
me had been dug up on his place and that they were of the Revolutionary
period.*

*The reef that extended East from this place . . . known as Wheatons point
was always a source of pleasure. . . . Here we used to go swimming. There
was comparatively deep water on the North side. At low tide when the water
was slack we would stand on the reef and dive down to the bottom, eight or ten
feet, and bring up flint pebbles. These pebbles ranged in size from one inch and
a half to six or eight. They were all approximately oval or round and many of
them broken open would display beautiful crystals formed in an interior cavity
of stone.*

*These flint stones were not indigenous to this locality, but were a part of the
cargo of a British vessel that was drifted on this reef by the force of the tide
during the Revolutionary war, and had to be lightened of her cargo before she
would float. These flints, of course, are sent over here from England for the
purpose of making flints for the locks of the muskets for the British troops.*

(In recent excavations near the foundations of Gracie Mansion some of
the flints were located.)

While Wheaton was working on additions to his property far uptown,
he was also expanding his business at a single new location at

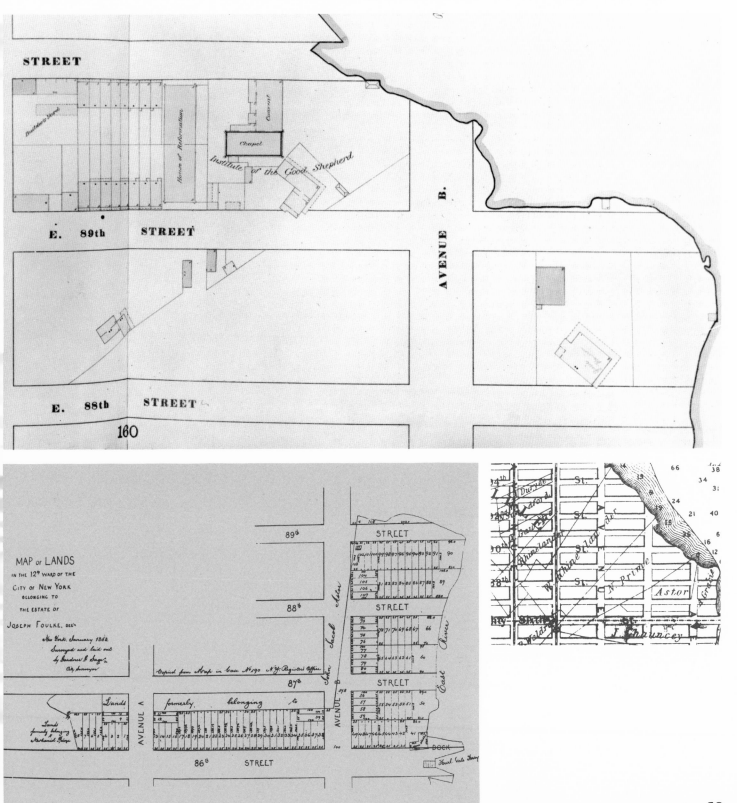

266 Canal Street (with changed street numbering, this shop was in the same block as his former shop on Canal Street), adding window glass and builder's hardware to millwork doors, sashes and blinds. This listing of his stock in Trow's 1855–56 directory, however, mirrors the debts outlined in a legal writ of 1859 directing that his entire estate, "real and personal of every nature kind and description" be turned over to accountant George A. Wheaton (who was probably his brother) and to Abram Wakeman, counselor at law with offices at No. 59 Fulton Street. He owed rent to John A. Bunting, an indication of the second mortgage on the Gracie property. By the end of 1859, the accountant and the attorney had worked out agreements to relieve Wheaton of "his financial embarrassments." Payment of his debts were to be made at fifty cents on the dollar. Gracie Mansion and the lots immediately surrounding it—already twice mortgaged—were the security for the settlement, administered by two of the creditors as trustees.

A view of Gracie Mansion dated that year (which appeared in *Valentine's Manual* of 1859) is taken from an angle that fails to reveal the new brick stable. The illustration shows the east side of the house, on a line with Hallett's Point in Astoria. There is a long, high picket fence along the 88th Street right of way. Another line of pickets parallel to the side porch appears to turn in front of the house and down the incline toward the water on the north side of Horn's Hook, the fencing descending the steep grade to the water. A small summer house, sketched in plan view in the 1870 real-estate atlas, is seen just below the crest of the rocky bank at river's edge.

While the appearance of Noah Wheaton's new stable is unknown, Archibald Gracie's massive old stone one on the East River just north of 86th Street is shown in an illustration of the Civil War period from the 1861 *Valentine's*. The subject of the print is the Hell Gate Ferry, the original Manhattan landing of the ferry to Astoria. Gracie's stable at water's edge adjoins a dock and has its own slip on the river, demonstrating the near certainty that it had been used throughout its history for storage and exchange of both land and water-borne cargo.

Two years after Wheaton's bankruptcy, the holder of the first mortgage on the property had not been paid, and the Great Western Insurance Company began foreclosure proceedings in December 1861. In late January, on payment of $10,000, the property reverted to the insurance company, although the family remained in the mansion as tenants.

Several portraits of the house and land and of the old ferry house date to the period of Grant's presidency. Three views of 1869, two of the

Harris' Point (Horen's Hook 1776), Wards Island and Hell Gate, 1859.
Lithograph by A. Weingartner, New York, for *D. T. Valentine's Manual*, 1859. *Gracie Mansion (at left) is seen from the south. The vista of the East River at Hell Gate also includes Hallett's Point on Long Island (now Astoria) at the extreme right of the print.*

Hell Gate Ferry–Foot of 86th Street, 1860.
Lithograph by Sarony, Major & Knapp, New York, for *D. T. Valentine's Manual, 1861.*
The view south from about the level of the 87th Street grid includes the Hell Gate Tavern and Archibald Gracie's old stone stable at center right. Blackwell's Island is seen across the East River at left center.

Gracie Lane, 86th Street and the East River.
Pen and ink on paper by Eliza Greatorex, 1869.
This rustic view shows the lane approach to the Astoria Ferry on Gracie land at about 86th Street. Through the opening in the trees the East River is seen. The rutted and overgrown roadway to the water provides evidence of its infrequent use after removal of the ferry landing to 92nd Street in 1866.

(top)
Gracie Mansion–View from Hell Gate.
Pen and ink on paper by Eliza Greatorex, 1869.
Taken from the river's edge at about 90th Street, Gracie Mansion shows obvious traces of neglect during the depressed years of the Wheaton family's occupancy.

(bottom)
Gracie Mansion.
Pen and ink on paper by Eliza Greatorex, 1869.
The main facade of Gracie Mansion is seen from the lawn, which fronts on the rocky ledge to the East River. Although the house was occupied by the Wheaton family, the closed shutters and overgrown shrubbery imply that it was vacant.

62

Old Hell-Gate Ferry House — 1867 B. Lander

Noah Wheaton's Advertisement.
New York *City Directory* 1870, opposite
p. 5.
*In 1870, Noah Wheaton appears to have had
increased success in his downtown enterprise in
architectural woodwork. Note the early use of
the word "refrigerators" in Wheaton's ad.*

Old Hell Gate Ferry House.
Pen and ink by Benjamin Lander, 1867.
*This is the old Hell Gate Tavern on the East
River shore at the foot of 86th Street, on land
now occupied by Carl Schurz Park.*

63

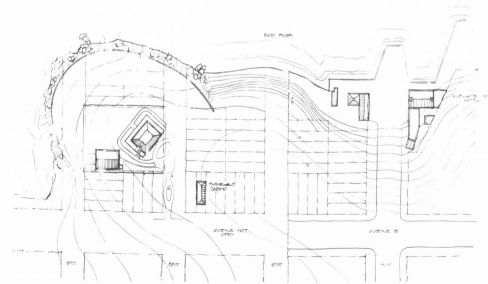

house and one of the hilly, rutted lane that led through tall trees on the 86th Street right of way, are by Eliza Greatorex. They are romantic, pastoral scenes that show wooded landscapes, tumble-down fences and a weathered house in need of paint. The far view of the house, probably sketched at or just south of 90th Street, shows an overgrown terrain with tall trees and the rough stone wall at the river shore at Horn's Hook, fallen and much altered from the laid river rock and cut stone seen in the similar vista of about 1810.

The Greatorex drawing of the entrance facade of the house, taken from the edge of the lawn, reveals its rundown condition, with woods and scrub growth closing in at the rear. The air of neglect is augmented by shuttered windows, although this may be misleading as the shutters on most windows in the neighborhood were opened and closed almost daily.

The rustic appearance of the area is reaffirmed by a 1867 drawing of the old Hell Gate Ferry House which illustrates a continuation of the wooded upland seen in the Greatorex view of 86th Street; it is rudely fenced at the edge of the former Gracie property, north of the lane to the old ferry.

Late in 1862, Wheaton defaulted on his mortgage for the water lot (seen in the foreground of the long-range Greatorex view), and the land was sold back to the mortgage holder, William Niblo, for $500. However, Wheaton children, grandchildren and friends continued to swim in this East River cove until the late 1880s when a sea wall and promenade were completed along the 89th Street right of way.

In 1869 and 1870, a distinct improvement occurred in Noah Wheaton's business and financial status. The directory of 1870 features a sizable advertisement for two of his stores on Canal Street. At No. 210 Canal, Wheaton sold doors in a store located in the large double six-story brick buildings at the corner of Mulberry Street. A few blocks west, at No. 268, was his shop where "refrigerators" were sold in the five-story brick structure one block east of Broadway. Another indicator of Wheaton's prosperity in 1870 was his repurchase of Gracie Mansion and the surrounding lots from the Great Western Insurance Company for $25,000.

The three Wheaton girls were now grown up. On September 25, 1873, the youngest, Alice Hermione (Hermie) Wheaton, then 24, was married to a 30-year-old lawyer, Lambert Suydam Quackenbush. The groom's father, pastor of Prospect Hill Reform Church, performed the ceremony. The Quackenbushes had been the Wheatons' neighbors since the latter's arrival in upper Manhattan, living in a handsome house at No. 231 East 86th Street, purchased in 1851 by Lambert Quackenbush's grandfather. After the marriage, the young couple

Gracie Mansion, 89th Street at the East River.
Pen and ink on cardboard by Abram Hosier, ca. 1870.
This view of Gracie Mansion from the southeast was drawn during the lean years of the Wheaton family occupancy. Like the Greatorex drawings of the same period, the house is seen amid an overgrown tangle of new growth in lots owned south of the mansion.

The Site—1870.
Pen and ink rendering by Philip N. Winslow, landscape architect, 1981.
This conjectural plan shows the topography and structures in the Horn's Hook area midway through Noah Wheaton's ownership of the land immediately surrounding Gracie Mansion.

stayed with the Wheatons at Gracie Mansion for five years, and the two oldest of their nine children, Amalie Hermione (Millie), and Daniel McLaren, were born there in 1875 and 1877, respectively.

In the spring of 1874 Wheaton took another mortgage on the Gracie site. By the end of that year he was again in financial hot water, and the house and lot once more became security to creditors. The cause of the bankruptcy was given: "losses, disappointments and other damages happened to Noah Wheaton." This time, one of the trustees (and one of the major creditors, as well) was his new son-in-law, Lambert S. Quackenbush. Besides the usual debts to merchants for sashes, glass and lumber, there were two large debts due to the milliner, Albert Shumway, for $10,327, and to Edward Le Comte, a dealer of feathers, for $6,772. The fact that Wheaton's two unmarried daughters were assignees, along with Quackenbush, may indicate that Wheaton's debts were being reassigned to his children as the means for repayment. The extraordinarily large debts to downtown merchants of feathers and millinery might be for loans directly to Noah Wheaton or to suppliers of hat forms, trimmings and feathers in a business enterprise conducted by Hettie and Jennie Wheaton, who continued to live at home.

In the year of the nation's centennial, two events occurred that were to change the appearance and use of the land and waters near Horn's Hook. The City of New York formally opened Avenue B from 77th to 83rd Street, and began construction of a small park in the land east and north of the new street. Directly across the river from Gracie Mansion the continuing attempt to clear the channel for safe shipping led to a complicated plan for demolition of the long reef at Hallett's Point. (It was there that the fort matching the one at Horn's Hook had been built by American soldiers in 1776.) Throughout the previous history of the mansion Hallett's Point and its reef had been landmarks easily identified from the lawn. On an autumn Sunday, nitroglycerine charges, placed under the reef by Cornish miners, were set off in "a gigantic water display," that Lyman assures us "was the talk of the town for months."

Lesser explosions were taking place, eroding Wheaton's 1870 prosperity. In 1877 Wheaton defaulted on his latest mortgage, and the Supreme Court of New York ordered the property sold. Although Noah Wheaton maintained in 1889 that he and his family had lived at Gracie Mansion continuously since 1857, there is no home address listed for him in the two city directories dated between 1878 and 1880. In 1878, Hermione and Lambert Quackenbush's residence is listed as being at No. 243 East 86th Street, near the latter's

childhood home. It is possible that this, the latest of Wheaton's business failures, sent the entire family from the house for a brief period. In 1878, Wheaton, recorded as a dealer in lumber, had a shop at a new location at No. 789 Broadway. In the directory for the following year, there is no entry for Noah Wheaton. He was 70 years old; in the years immediately following, directory listings are only for his residence at Gracie Mansion, except for 1882 to 1883 when he is listed as a "merchant" at his home address.

That the Wheatons were living in the mansion in 1879 is indicated in *New York in 1809* by Charles King (the widower of Eliza Gracie), published 70 years later in the *Magazine of American History*. It is noted there, in an article on Archibald Gracie and his family, that "the old building and the point are now in possession of Mr. N. Wheaton, who resides on the place." The neighborhood was changing as the city continued its northward expansion. In 1881 construction began on 24 picturesque Queen Anne style houses on the west side of Avenue B between 87th and 89th Streets "for people of moderate means." In 1886, the year in which the Statue of Liberty was dedicated in New York Harbor, Parks Department President Henry E. Beekman announced plans for further expansion of East River Park, noting a trend in the Gracie Mansion vicinity:

The importance of extending it to the north and largely increasing its area is obvious, not only for artistic reasons, but also for the better accommodation of the thousands now using the park and a proper provision for the rapidly increasing population of this part of the city.

In 1884, as Jane Wheaton married the real-estate broker Hamlin Babcock, the condition of both the house and the family's finances improved. After their marriage the Babcocks lived at Gracie Mansion, Hamlin Babcock listing "the foot of 88th Street" as his home from 1882 to 1896, and as the location of his real-estate business in directories from 1893 to 1896. In 1885, apparently freed from the demands of running a hardware or millwork store, Noah Wheaton served as contractor for a number of improvements to the mansion. New pipes to the existing furnace in the basement were installed between the floor beams, and about a quarter of the flooring on the long porch was replaced with new oak; the following year a tin roof was installed.

In 1888, Babcock set into motion a Supreme Court suit and several appeals that eventually led to transfer of the house and lots to him on July 22, 1892. At the same time some work had progressed on the first section of East River Park south of 86th Street, as hearings were begun to secure the land north to 89th Street. In their final report,

Tintype of Wheaton Family Members on the Lawn in Front of Gracie Mansion, ca. 1890.
As nearly as can be determined, the Wheaton family relations assembled on the lawn in front of Gracie Mansion in early spring are, from left to right: Jenny (or Jane) Wheaton Babcock; her nephew, Daniel McLaren Quackenbush; her niece, Olive Quackenbush; another niece, Nathalie; her husband, Hamlin Babcock; her oldest niece, Amalie Hermione (Millie) Quackenbush; her mother, Amelia Ball Wheaton; and her sister, Esther Wheaton. The balustrade around the eaves (the first thing to go when the city took over the property in 1896) is secured by stays attached to the roof.

Double photographs of members of the Wheaton Family.
Photograph by S. C. Levison, "Amtr" with "The Brainerd Hand Camera," late 1880s.
These charming photographs of Wheaton Family members record the appearance of Noah Wheaton and his wife (to the right in the right-hand group of four) and his daughters and their husbands (left photo, left to right: Lambert S. Quackenbush, husband of Alice Hermione Wheaton; Jane Wheaton, next to her husband, former New York Councilman Hamlin Babcock). In the right photo a Wheaton cousin, Harriet Noyes, far left, stands next to Esther Wheaton, the unmarried daughter in the family. These family records were taken from the lawn in front of Gracie Mansion; the public promenade built in the late 1880s is seen in the background. The right photo reveals the yacht landing west of Gracie Mansion on the East River inlet above 90th Street, and beyond it a vessel of the Astoria ferry line which then operated from a slip at 92nd Street.

Gracie Mansion, Main Facade.
Photograph by Pach Brothers, New York,
ca. 1890.
*Three generations of Wheaton family women
were photographed on the front lawn of Gracie
Mansion in the early 1890s. The little girl
with the croquet mallet is probably Olive
Whedon Quackenbush (b. 1885); her aunt,
Esther Wheaton, is seated under a tree facing
her mother, Amelia Ball Wheaton (Mrs.
Noah Wheaton). The lady seated on the porch
is the child's mother, Alice Hermione Wheaton
Quackenbush.*

Gracie Mansion from East End Avenue.
Photograph by Pach Brothers, New York,
ca. 1890.
*The two-story ell that housed the service stair
may be seen in this view of Gracie Mansion
late in the Wheaton occupancy. Brick paving
went under the porch, canted slightly to the
outer periphery of the porch; it probably served
as a run-off for any moisture that might have
collected near the base of the house. The
gardens, trees and view of the river from the
house had been famous since Gracie's day; the
opulent late garden of the Wheatons hints at
its wonder.*

Gracie Mansion from the Rear.
Photograph by Pach Brothers, New York, ca. 1890.
This vista of Gracie Mansion was taken from about the level of 87th Street at present East End Avenue, now the northernmost section of Carl Schurz Park. The picket fence and handsome pedestrian and carriage gates mark the southern boundary of the Wheatons' property. The crude angled fence of stakes with one course of wire shows the Wheatons' use of the property south of the mansion for the family driveway. The small bearded figure at the pedestrian gate is unidentified, but he serves to show the quite heroic scale of the two gates.

Gracie Mansion, West Elevation.
Photograph by Pach Brothers, New York, ca. 1890.
Olive Whedon Quackenbush, the daughter of Lambert Suydam Quackenbush and his wife, Alice Hermione Wheaton, poses with her dog at the back of Gracie Mansion (near the kitchen entrance at the northwest corner of the building).

Main Hall, View West—Gracie Mansion during the Wheaton Occupancy.
Photograph by Pach Brothers, New York, ca. 1890.
Nowhere is the Wheaton enthusiasm for pattern more visible than in the entrance hall of Gracie Mansion. The painting of the young girl at right portrays Amalie Hermione Quackenbush, granddaughter of Noah Wheaton who occupied the Mansion from 1855 to 1893. The left-hand portrait is of a Wheaton daughter who died before the family moved into the house.

dated November 1, 1890, the Parks Commissioners pronounced themselves unable to determine the ownership of Gracie Mansion and the water lots adjoining it to the east. Hamlin Babcock filed objections to this finding in Supreme Court, saying that the "award made to unknown owners for the said parcel" was "insufficient," and further objected that the award "should have been made to him as owner thereof."

Babcock was able to show that the last purchaser of record owned only a partial mortgage on the property and not the land itself. He was eventually declared the owner, was awarded $63,500 for its purchase for park use and was ordered to pay off the mortgage. In the summer of 1892 Babcock finally secured clear title as the house and 12 lots were transferred to him.

Until 1896 both the Wheatons and the Babcocks listed their residence as the foot of East 88th Street. In 1893 and 1894, Noah Wheaton, 85 years old, was listed as being in the real-estate business with an office in the Bronx at No. 126 Alexander Avenue. The following year, and to the year 1896, when he died, he listed the foot of East 88th Street, not only as his home, but also as the location for his real-estate office.

In a double photograph of adult members of the Wheaton family and their in-laws taken in the early 1890s by T. C. Levison, an "amateur photographer" (according to the stamp on the back), the family are posed on the lawn of Gracie Mansion. Very clearly, work had proceeded on the northern extension of the park. A promenade had been built at the top of a new retaining wall, with an iron fence at the river's edge that followed the line immediately north of the 89th Street grid. In the inlet of the river beyond Horn's Hook, sailboats were anchored just below the foot of 90th Street. At center left was the Astoria ferry slip at 92nd Street.

A tintype of the same period shows four of the Quackenbush elders and four of their children posed with a hoop, badminton racket and other toys on Gracie Mansion lawn. The land behind the house was clear of shrubbery and trees, either in preparation for the park extension or in the first stages of its landscaping. The elegant railing surmounting the house at the eave line was secured to the roof with supports behind each urn finial.

But sometime after 1890 and before the Wheatons and the Babcocks left the Mansion in 1896, Pach Brothers Photographers were called in to record the exterior of the freshly painted house, tidy fence, flourishing gardens, neatly trimmed trees and shrubbery and exuberant late Victorian decor and furnishings of the interior.

The contrast between inside and out is remarkable. Much of the
furniture and all the wallpaper date to the late 1880s and early 1890s.
In the study and parlor, oriental rugs are laid over figured carpets,
while in the hall they lie on linoleum or a painted floorcloth. The
fireplace in the hall is walled in, and a Victorian newel post and stair
balusters have replaced the originals. A patent platform rocker by
George Hunzinger has a place of honor in the study. Heavy draperies
enfold doors and closets, and embroidered muslin and lace curtains
flutter at the windows. The fireplaces have drawn curtains as draft
covers, and an 1870 Rogers Group, *Coming to the Parson*, occupies a
place of honor in the parlor. Oriental fans, a print of Lincoln and his
cabinet, a bust of Washington after Houdon, elegant gilt mirrors, two
family portraits and several landscapes in oil attest to the prosperity
of the Wheaton household in its last years in Archibald Gracie's lovely
mansion.

(top and bottom)
***Parlor–Gracie Mansion during the
Wheaton Occupancy.***
Photographs by Pach Brothers, New
York, ca. 1890.
*Two views of the present large drawing room of
Gracie Mansion demonstrate the Wheatons'
enthusiasm for late Victorian style. One of the
hundreds of plaster castings of John Rogers'
Coming to the Parson may be seen under the
oval mirror; the walls are hung with a
fascinating collection of landscapes. The
portrait and genre painter George Henry Story
had an introduction to the family and it is
possible that some of the paintings are his. In
the corner on the opposite wall is a plaster cast
of Washington that appears to be modeled after
one by Houdon. Remarkable indeed are the
ailanthus branches (probably pruned from the
lots adjoining the Wheatons' property) in large
vases.*

Study, Northeast View—Gracie Mansion during the Wheaton Occupancy.
Photograph by Pach Brothers, New York, ca. 1890.
The pattern-on-pattern Victorian ebullience of the decor late in the Wheatons' occupancy of Gracie Mansion is seen in this view of the study. To the left of the draped table is a patent rocker by George Hunzinger. The furniture and wallpaper pattern all date to the late nineteenth century and serve to show the prosperity that came to the Wheaton family at the end of the 39-year stay at the present Mayor's House of New York.

Dining Room, Northeast View— Gracie Mansion during the Wheaton Occupancy.
Photograph by Pach Brothers, New York, ca. 1890.
The asymmetrical plan of the living room, its off-center fireplace and chandelier, and the curious interior fanlight above the door between the dining room and central hall are emphasized in this view. The restoration architects who are planning the renovation of the mansion believe that there was once a matching door on the opposite wall which was the original axis of the house, with the front door facing the river rather than the inlet of Horn's Hook, its entrance since the early nineteenth century.

Gracie Mansion as a Public Building, 1896–1943

Beginning in 1888, and off and on in the two years that followed, hearings were continued to determine the owners of the East River land north of 86th Street. Clear title was secured by the Wheaton family in the summer of 1892. Despite city condemnation proceedings begun for park use in 1891, the family remained in the mansion. At last, in 1896, a year in which the nation's twenty-fifth President, William McKinley, was elected, the Wheaton family, who had lived at the house at Horn's Hook longer than any other, ended their residence, leaving behind a house in good repair, its interior fashionably papered over every inch of available wall and ceiling.

From 1896 until 1942, for even longer than the Wheatons' stay, the house was in the hands of the New York Parks Commission. Often, in the 46 years in which family life was absent, it was neglected, its rooms and lawn haunted by the gaiety and laughter that had been its charms when the large Gracie, Foulke and Wheaton families lived there. A memory remained. Later, a resident mayor—misreading an 1875 date as 1815—capriciously identified the "Millie" whose name was etched on a pane in the study, as a "girl friend of Archibald Gracie's." The ghosts knew better. Millie was Amalie Hermione Quackenbush, her name etched on the glass in 1893 by her brother, with a diamond ring, an eighteenth-birthday gift of their father.

As New York's Department of Parks landscaped the north section of East River Park, the high fence with its handsome gate and gateposts was removed. Park benches were installed along the promenade encircling the mansion, and several slender, metal-dome-topped street lamps, in general use throughout the city, were erected to shed evening light on the walk at the river's edge. By 1904, the elegant chinoiserie rail around the roof, secured by wood supports in the mid-1890s, was removed. In less than three years, second-floor shutters and the railing above the porch, falling apart and with missing elements, was taken down, leaving the house looking forlorn and neglected.

Even though the mansion was suffering from disuse, this area of East River Park was valued at $1,826,000 in 1908. Now renamed in honor of Carl Schurz, the new designation honored not only the German revolutionary, American diplomat, cabinet member and editor of both the *New York Evening Post* and *Harper's Weekly*, but also the growing German population of Yorkville, where Schurz had settled in 1881. This 1911 identification of part of the land that had once been Archibald Gracie's was an inadvertent bow to its early owner, as Gracie had helped to organize the *Evening Post* 110 years earlier.

By 1913, despite attempts to maintain the house for Department of Parks' use, Noah Wheaton's blinds were falling apart; the flooring and many of the windows were broken (although "Millie" etched in the study pane remained). The Department of Parks prepared plans for "Restoration of Gracie Mansion in Carl Schurz Park." Gas and electric lights, floor heating registers, a toilet on the second floor and almost all the closets were to be removed. Mantels, hearths, wood trim, cornices and interior shutters were to be repaired and new floors and a new lighting system were planned. Best of all, the chinoiserie railings were to be rebuilt and the whole place painted. It was a hopeful plan on paper by architect Julius Kraus, but the only real work done in 1913 was the planting of shrubbery and plane trees in Carl Schurz Park.

Two years later, in *Old Roads from the Heart of New York*, Sarah Comstock recorded useful activity at Gracie Mansion in sewing classes for girls and a carpentry shop for boys, held "in a small part of its spaciousness." A city guide of the following year noted its use as a refreshment stand where ices and soda water were sold, with comfort stations in the basement serving visitors to Carl Schurz Park.

Some repairs were made in the early 1920s, and the exterior received an extraordinary coat of fresh paint in "tan color with red trimmings."

In 1923 the last of three bills presented to the State Legislature for the preservation, use and maintenance of "the old historic building known as Gracie Mansion" was passed. The two unsuccessful measures that preceded it called for turning the mansion over to Patriotic New Yorkers, an organization headed by May King Van Rensselaer, Archibald Gracie's great-granddaughter. As Mrs. John King, she was known as a writer on subjects as diverse as crochet lace, nonsuch euchre and other games, and of a gossipy romp through New York life called *Our Social Ladder*. A *New York Times* article which appeared two days after her death was hardly flattering to the lady's vigorous efforts on behalf of her ancestor:

She kept alive the inherited prejudice against Washington Irving, whose "Knickerbocker History" was resented by old New Yorkers in whom pride of race was greater than sense of humor . . . Her knowledge of New York was never so profound as that of her relative Mrs. Schuyler Van Rensselaer. Nor did she approach the scholarship of Isaac Newton Phelps Stokes.

From 1915 to 1920, May King Van Rensselaer, described as looking like "a Duchess of the Victorian period," had assertively waged war on the New-York Historical Society in an effort to enliven what she

East 86th Street and East River Park
with Gracie Mansion at the North End.
Photograph by Jacob Riis, ca. 1906.

Gracie Mansion in Carl Schurz Park.
Photograph, ca. 1906.

Gracie Mansion.
Photograph by an unidentified photographer, early twentieth century. *The shorn and naked mansion, without the elegant Chinese Chippendale eave and porch balustrades, missing the shutters on the second-floor windows, shows its sad decline early in its ownership by the city. The porch roof is bolstered into line by the four square pillars at either side of the front entrance where the Wheatons' Victorian rail and stair posts are still to be seen. Lattices have been installed to hide the area under the porch that was used for storage in this period.*

Map of Manhattan Island in 1908, Vol. 2, Sections 5 & 6 (detail).
G. W. Bromley & Co., New York, 1908. *The growth and development of the city in the early twentieth century is illustrated in this map that shows Carl Schurz Park (lower left), in its early years, with Gracie Mansion at the north end of the park. The house, owned by the city, was used as a refreshment stand and storage-and-office space for the park.*

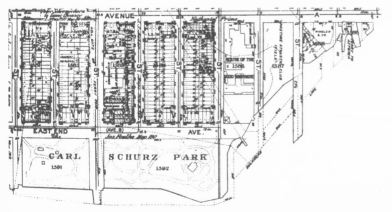

called an "old man's club" with a series of teas under her sponsorship, and the installation there of period rooms and memorial windows. Twice threatening practical jokes in retribution if her schemes were not accepted, Mrs. Van Rensselaer's suggestions were finally tabled in referral to the society's Executive Committee. Unsuccessful at turning the society around, she channeled her energies into backing "a movement to have the Archibald Gracie Mansion at Horen Hook, Hellsgate, opened as a historical museum, under the patronage of twenty society women, representatives of the oldest families in New York." Her plans were "to install figures of men and women—call them wax figures, if you like—dressed in costumes of their times, and surrounded by the furniture they knew."

The defeat of the two bills for a museum at Gracie Mansion that were linked to her Patriotic New Yorkers, and the passage of the bill in which they were not mentioned, appears as a rejection of the restoration and presentation program that she proposed. The bill, published in the state law of 1923, called for the establishment of a museum in Gracie Mansion, "affording to the public opportunities for pleasure, recreation, amusement and education by means of the exhibition of the said building and its contents." In April 1923, Mayor John F. Hylan announced his support of the measure's provisions, and Henry Collins Brown, then editor of *Valentine's Manual*, was made managing director of the new city museum.

Mrs. Van Rensselaer continued to pull at her end of the rope in a genteel tug of war to have the historic house placed in the custody of the Society of Patriotic New Yorkers. She reported that she owned some of the Gracie furniture and would place it in the house if her proposal was successful. In June, the *New York Times*, under the headline "Gracie Mansion Is in Dispute—Two Societies Seek Use of Historic House in Carl Schurz Park"—gave details of the struggle and announced the first meeting of the museum's incorporators.

The founding trustees did not include Mrs. John King Van Rensselaer, but did include her relation by marriage, Mrs. Schuyler Van Rensselaer, herself the author of the two-volume *History of the City of New York in the Seventeenth Century*, published in 1909. Incorporation took place toward the end of July, and the museum was given a lease for the house by the Commissioner of Parks on October 10, 1923, with Henry Collins Brown's *Valentine's Manual* serving as its official year book. The city was to provide the building, keep it in repair and maintain the grounds, while the museum would be responsible for care of collections and providing funds for a working staff.

Late in the year, Brown announced that sponsorship of the museum at Gracie Mansion had been reorganized, as the Museum of the City of New York came into being. Its first formal meeting was held in the mansion on December 18. While the *Times* reported that the "marks" of the "Many tenants since Gracie are disappearing," the only specific notice of change referred to the hall: "Inside, the wide hall of Colonial spaciousness is being restored to its former simplicity." This, and a flurry of activity including "a great refurbishing of faded paint and buried fireplaces," might indicate that some fireplaces had been blocked off by Wheaton or the Parks Department for a central heating system. (The discreet curtains drawn over them in the Pach Brothers' photographs of the early 1890s hide the evidence of their use late in the Wheaton occupancy.) Illustrations in *Valentine's Manual* of 1924 show that Victorian, marine and print rooms– among others– were installed. The layer of tan and red paint seems to have been painted over, although there were no other exterior improvements.

The museum opened to the public on November 7, 1924–the year in which Calvin Coolidge was nominated. Shortly after, the fragile nature of the old frame house was discussed and alternative sites for the museum were suggested, including one of the Vanderbilt mansions on Fifth Avenue and a plot assembled on Washington Square South. In 1926, the second director of the museum, Hardinge Scholle, toured European historic sites and museums as his trustees recognized that Gracie Mansion was neither large enough nor central enough to be a satisfactory permanent home for the Museum of the City of New York.

While an exhibition to raise funds for a permanent location was on view at the Fine Arts Building on West 57th Street, Gracie Mansion was "restored to its original condition." The restoration included some work on the porch railings and replacement of "ornate railings" along the roof eave and the porch. The exterior was painted once more; the walls were white and the shutters green.

Period decoration and furnishing of the rooms took place as the restoration was completed. The hall was furnished in Sheraton style and a Victorian room of 1850 was installed, complete with a marble mantel on loan to the museum. The central drawing room on the second floor was dedicated to the memory of Mrs. John King Van Rensselaer. Among other furnishings in the room was a card table, once owned by Dr. David Hosack, the physician and botanist. In the *Times* article announcing the official reopening of the museum on March 21, 1927, it was noted that Alexander Hamilton, Philip Hone and Archibald Gracie were among those who had played cards at Dr. Hosack's table.

(above)
Gracie Mansion.
Photograph, 1923.
*This view of the main facade of the mansion
was taken during the year of its designation as
a museum. The exterior at this time was
painted tan with red trim.*

(left)

Gracie Mansion.
Photograph by Byron Co., New York,
ca. 1923–1927.
*On December 4, 1923, director Henry Collins
Brown declared that Gracie Mansion had
recently been turned over "to the newly
organized Museum of the City of New York."
The Museum was opened to the public on
November 7, 1924. In 1926 a fund-raising
campaign for a new building was begun.
Meanwhile, a refurbished Gracie Mansion
was reopened to the public on March 21,*
*1927. The museum moved to its new structure
at Fifth Avenue and East 103rd Street in
August 1932, leaving Gracie Mansion
unoccupied.*

(above)

Gracie Mansion.
Watercolor by Rudolph F. Bunner
(1860–1931), 1928.
*The modern-day mayor's house is seen in a
period in which it was in use as the first home
of the Museum of the City of New York.*

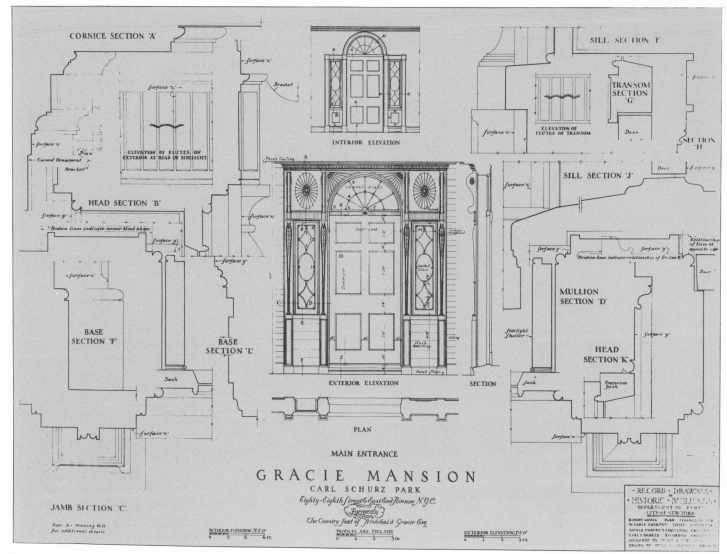

GRACIE MANSION

CARL SCHURZ PARK

Eighty-Eighth Street & East End Avenue N.Y.C.

Formerly

The Country Seat of Archibald Gracie Esq.

Record Drawings of Gracie Mansion.
Historic American Building Survey,
1935.

*Drawings of Gracie Mansion show the
building as it was surveyed in 1935 in record
drawings ordered by Park Commissioner
Robert Moses, who in 1942 persuaded Mayor
Fiorello La Guardia to designate Archibald
Gracie's lovely old East River home as the
official residence of New York's mayors.*

84

Carl Schurz Park and Gracie Mansion.
New York Times, April 21, 1940.
*Carl Schurz Park and the shore of the East
River are seen in this photograph showing
construction of the East River Drive north of
87th Street. The proximity of the highway
tunnel to Gracie Mansion and its position
under the lawn are also illustrated in this
view.*

Gracie Mansion.
Oil on canvas by Isabella R. Markell, ca. 1940.

Seen from on high over Carl Schurz Park, at about the level of 87th Street, Gracie Mansion is dwarfed by the Triborough and Harlem Railroad Bridges. Yet its orientation toward the River and Hell Gate is clear, one of the marvels endlessly noted by visitors from Archibald Gracie's time to the present.

Less than two weeks after the reopening of Gracie Mansion by the Museum of the City of New York, Governor Alfred E. Smith signed a measure empowering the city's Board of Estimate to provide a new site for the museum. Three years later came the selection of a building site at Fifth Avenue and 103th Street. By August 1932, Gracie Mansion was unoccupied once more, as the museum moved to its permanent home.

In 1934, Park Commissioner Robert Moses relocated the Welfare Island ferry from 86th Street to 78th so that the two sections of Carl Schurz Park might be joined. That same year he ordered another restoration of Gracie Mansion under consulting architect Aymar Embury, II, and Chief Engineer W. Earle Andrews.

A new roof, new clapboards, new ornamental railings and a rebuilt porch were among the exterior improvements. While the public comfort facilities in the basement were retained, a number of structural changes took place inside, as a door between the dining room and pantry was closed to accommodate two lavatories; the Wheatons' Victorian newel post and stair rails were replaced by ones of colonial design.

In the spring of 1936, this careful restoration was complete, and the house was furnished with collections of fine American furniture on loan from the Metropolitan Museum of Art, the Museum of the City of New York and collector Francis P. Garvan, who loaned "six pieces valued at more than $15,000." Mrs. Mary Gracie Higginson, granddaughter of Archibald Gracie, loaned some of her ancestor's furniture to the mansion as the new house museum was opened to the public early in May 1936.

The penultimate step in topographical changes to Archibald Gracie's land took place in the late thirties and early forties as the Franklin D. Roosevelt Drive was constructed beneath the broad promenade along the waterfront (now John H. Finlay Walk). The road tunnels through the rise on which the mansion stands, only a few feet from the house itself. Even as the East River Drive was set in place beneath Carl Schurz Park, Robert Moses proposed the present use of Archibald Gracie's country seat. Mayor La Guardia at first resisted the idea, but eventually, his widow recalls, "Bob Moses wore him down." The La Guardias became the first mayoral family to inhabit the newly designated official residence, the last of the many miracles that preserved for New Yorkers this house and point of land at Horn's Hook overlooking the churning waters of Hell Gate.

87

Mayors of the
City of New York

1 Thomas Willett, 1662
2 Thomas Delavall, 1665
3 Thomas Willett, 1666
4 Cornelius Steenwyck, 1668–1670
5 Thomas Delavall, 1671
6 Matthias Nicolls, 1672
7 John Lawrence, 1673
8 William Dervall, 1675
9 Nicholas De Meyer, 1676
10 Stephanus Van Cortlandt, 1677
11 Thomas Delavall, 1678
12 Francis Rombouts, 1679
13 William Dyre, 1680–1681
14 Cornelius Steenwyck, 1682–1683
15 Gabriel Minvielle, 1684
16 Nicholas Bayard, 1685
17 Stephanus Van Cortlandt,
    1686–1688
18 Peter Delanoy, 1689–1690
19 John Lawrence, 1691
20 Abraham De Peyster, 1692–1694
21 Charles Lodwik, 1694–1695
22 William Merrett, 1695–1698
23 Johannes De Peyster, 1698–1699
24 David Provost, 1699–1700
25 Isaac de Reimer, 1700–1701
26 Thomas Noell, 1701–1702
27 Philip French, 1702–1703
28 William Peartree, 1703–1707
29 Ebenezer Wilson, 1707–1710
30 Jacobus Van Cortlandt, 1710–1711
31 Caleb Heathcote, 1711–1714
32 John Johnson, 1714–1719
33 Jacobus Van Cortlandt, 1719–1720
34 Robert Walters, 1720–1725
35 Johannes Jansen, 1725–1726
36 Robert Lurling, 1726–1735
37 Paul Richard, 1735–1739
38 John Cruger, 1739–1744
39 Stephen Bayard, 1744–1747
40 Edward Holland, 1747–1757
41 John Cruger, Jr., 1757–1766
42 Whitehead Hicks, 1766–1776
43 David Mathews, 1776–1784
44 James Duane, 1784–1789
45 Richard Varick, 1789–1801
46 Edward Livingston, 1801–1803
47 De Witt Clinton, 1803–1807
48 Marinus Willett, 1807–1808
49 De Witt Clinton, 1808–1810
50 Jacob Radcliff, 1810–1811
51 De Witt Clinton, 1811–1815
52 John Ferguson, 1815
53 Jacob Radcliff, 1815–1818
54 Cadwallader D. Colden, 1818–1821

55 Stephen Allen, 1821–1824
56 William Paulding, 1825–1826
57 Philip Hone, 1826–1827
58 William Paulding, 1827–1829
59 Walter Browne, 1829–1833
60 Gideon Lee, 1833–1834
61 Cornelius W. Lawrence, 1834–1837
62 Aaron Clark, 1837–1839
63 Isaac L. Varian, 1839–1841
64 Robert H. Morris, 1841–1844
65 James Harper, 1844–1845
66 William F. Havemeyer, 1845–1846
67 Andrew H. Mickle, 1846–1847
68 William V. Brady, 1847–1848
69 William F. Havemeyer, 1848–1849
70 Caleb S. Woodhull, 1849–1851
71 Ambrose C. Kingsland, 1851–1853
72 Jacob A. Westervelt, 1853–1855
73 Fernando Wood, 1855–1858
74 Daniel F. Tieman, 1858–1860
75 Fernando Wood, 1860–1862
76 George Opdyke, 1862–1864
77 C. Godfrey Gunther, 1864–1866
78 John T. Hoffman, 1866–1868
    T. Coman (Acting Mayor), 1868
79 A. Oakey Hall, 1869–1872
80 William F. Havemeyer, 1873–1874
    S.B.H. Vance (Acting Mayor), 1874
81 William H. Wickham, 1875–1876
82 Smith Ely, 1877–1878
83 Edward Cooper, 1879–1880
84 William R. Grace, 1881–1882
85 Franklin Edson, 1883–1884
86 William R. Grace, 1885–1886
87 Abram S. Hewitt, 1887–1888
88 Hugh J. Grant, 1889–1892
89 Thomas F. Gilroy, 1893–1894
90 William L. Strong, 1895–1897
91 Robert A. Van Wyck, 1898–1901
92 Seth Low, 1902–1903
93 George B. McClellan, 1904–1909
94 William J. Gaynor, 1910–1913
    Ardolph L. Kline (Acting Mayor),
    1913
95 John Purroy Mitchel, 1914–1917
96 John F. Hylan, 1918–1925
97 James J. Walker, 1926–1932*
    Joseph V. McKee (Acting Mayor),
    1932
98 John P. O'Brien, 1933
99 Fiorello H. LaGuardia, 1934–1945
100 William O'Dwyer, 1946–1950**
101 Vincent R. Impellitteri,
     1950–1953***
102 Robert F. Wagner, 1954–1965

103 John V. Lindsay, 1966–1973
104 Abraham D. Beame, 1974–1977
105 Edward I. Koch, 1978–

*Resigned Sept. 1, 1932
**Resigned Sept. 2, 1950
***Acting Mayor from Sept. 2, 1950 to
   Nov. 14, 1950; elected Nov. 7, 1950.

Index

The Gracie Mansion Conservancy, a not-for-profit corporation, was established in 1981 by Mayor Edward I. Koch to preserve and enhance the landmark house and its grounds for the benefit of the people of the City of New York. The members of its Board of Directors are:

Designed by Peter Laundy, Vignelli Associates
Printed by John D. Lucas Printing Company
Produced by Publishing Center for Cultural Resources

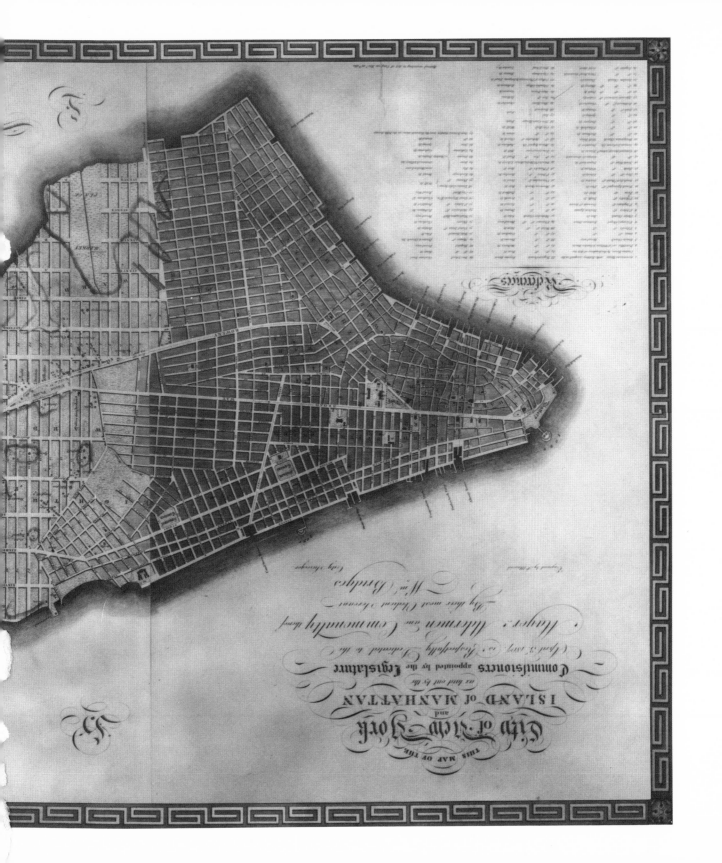

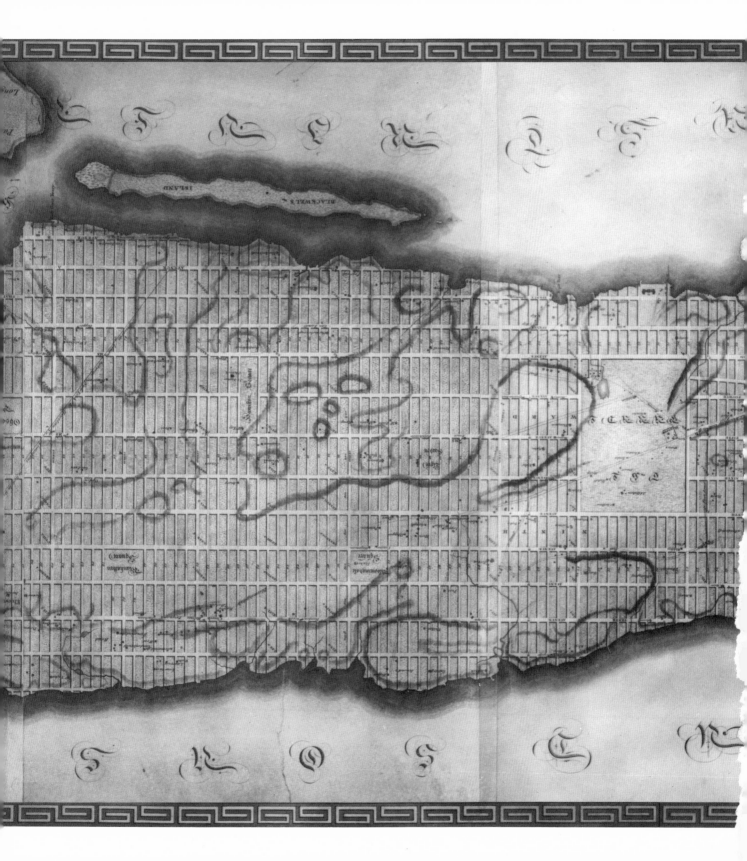

Foldout map overleaf

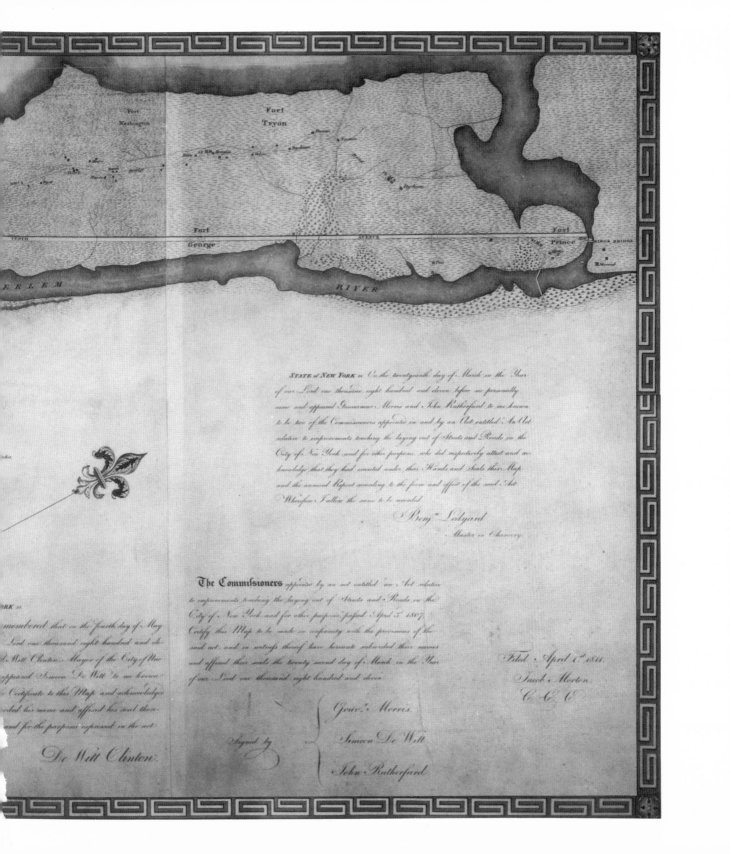

Map of the City of New York and Island of Manhattan as laid out by the Commissioners Appointed by the Legislature April 3rd, 1807, from the original survey by John Randel, Jr., 1811.

Engraving by Peter Maverick.

Marinus Willet was mayor of New York on April 3, 1807, when the commission was established to draw up this street map of Manhattan. De Witt Clinton succeeded Willet as mayor in 1807 and still held this office in 1811 when the delineation was complete. Archibald Gracie's downtown residence was located on State Street between Bridge and Pearl Streets facing the Battery. Although not noted on this map (Gracie's townhouse was completed in 1812), his country estate on Horn's Hook at Avenue B (East End Avenue) and 88th Street is marked with his name.

Scale of One Mile.